CONFESSIONS OF A BARISTA

On Platform 1

Joanna Murray

The
Firle
Press

First Published in Great Britain in 2021 by The Firle Press

www.thefirlepress.co.uk

A CIP catalogue record for this book is available from the British Library

PB ISBN 978-1-8382873-0-6

EB ISBN 978-1-8382873-1-3

Cover Designer – Tim Barber – www.dissectdesigns.com

Author Photograph – www.sarahtate.co.uk

Typesetting by Book Polishers

Dedicated to my greatest achievements

Sebastian, Tatiana and Hamish.

"Dream large and never be afraid to ride your own train."

Disclaimer: Please note that whilst this is a true story, in order to preserve the privacy of the many people who have trusted me with intimate details of their lives, I have changed certain identifying details.

Please also note that everything in these pages was told to me in a public setting, where anyone passing could stop and listen (and sometimes did, either overtly or while taking far too long deciding which coffee to buy).

Contents

Chapter 1

Coffee

How AND WHEN you take it speaks volumes about you and I.

'Coffee?' Such an innocent but loaded question. Coffee – the elixir of my soul and many others.

'Would you like a coffee?' – a social enhancer – encouraging people to be civil – friendly even – either through the comforting ritual of consumption or the effect of the drink itself. Coffee – the code breaker for antisocial silence.

'Coffee?' A question I ask a hundred times a day since I opened the coffee shop on Platform 1 at St Leonards Warrior Square Station. I have, inadvertently, become an observer to the hidden power behind a cup of it. Let me explain.

I have discovered that in the time it takes to make a coffee, strangers feel liberated enough to open up a secret window to their own souls. They sip and share. Intimate details tumble out – personal validations supporting their individual life stories.

I have also discovered that on the surface – we all show our 'every day' to the world in practical monochrome – but one small scratch reveals a myriad of colour. This is a journey of discovery.

"The train now approaching platform 1 is the 06.05 Southeastern Service (blue train) to London Charing Cross…"

Civil Dawn

THE SUN IS 6 degrees below the horizon. The early summer sunrise teases the Station into life. The booking hall box office is open. Stig, station staff for Southeastern (blue trains), is sitting behind his counter, window blind up – ready to sell tickets to commuters for the performance of their day. *"Morning Stig."* I call out every day on my way through to my coffee shop, whether there is a queue or not, whether he hears me or not. I call out because I believe small acknowledgments are hugely important – I wish more passengers felt the same way.

I hurry down Platform 1 – London side – St Leonards Warrior Square Station. Bag slung over my shoulder, arms tasked with the safe delivery of 24 pints of milk – 12 in each hand – my personal best – it's the awkwardness of the grip – rather than weight that makes safe delivery precarious. I am strong. I like a challenge.

As I unlock the door I can hear the tannoy droning on in superior monotone. Monotone – even the word sounds dull. I have a musical ear – preferring an arrangement of tones – rather than a semibreve on repeat. A semibreve is actually a fabulous name for a type of coffee – I shall invent it!

I am always early – ahead of the tannoy's schedule. I hate being late – time anxiety? – possibly. If I lose an hour in the morning I know I will spend the rest of the day looking for it. I prefer to run on time – perhaps I should have operated the railway rather than the coffee shop. Opening on time matters to me and my customers. That said, I find the phrase 'time management' distasteful – so corporate – so restrictive – and just by saying it you are likely to overwhelm yourself with self-inflicted feelings of panic to 'manage' your time – which will after all – inevitably tick by on its own.

I accept the fact that some kind of daily routine is important – of course it is – because we function better as a society when we all have some idea of what we are doing and when we are doing it. A necessary infrastructure framework of o'clock rules is in place for the common good – whether I like it or not. I learnt to run ahead of time at a young age – understanding that getting ahead is the fastest route to 'free time' – that heavenly state of playground existence where the free-spirited roam.

For those yet to visit St Leonards on Sea – it is a coastal town with a diverse nature and rising class status. It strives and struggles to blend tolerance and creativity into an ongoing turbulent mix of social deprivation versus gentrification. It remains unbalanced. The Station is used by all walks of life – the intrinsic nature of public transport. The coffee shop serves as a place to observe, capturing attitudes and behaviours which, in turn, form snapshot glimpses into everyday lives. It is true that 'a society's greatness is defined by how it treats its weakest members.' St Leonards has its share.

Door open, lights on, milk safely in fridges, I grab a stainless-steel jug and conduct my own dawn chorus with the steam wand – timed to perfection – the shot hits the cup – the wand starts to hiss – and the first pour of the day is mine – always – no exception – I need it to function. Two sips, I don't gulp – it's rude, on my way round to drag the Lavazza pavement signs on to the platform.

Signage out – I look across and see Stig in the flowerbed on Platform 2. Strange.

"Everything alright Stig?" Then I see the body – just lying there amongst the plantings of the Community Garden.

"Not sure," he says, standing apprehensively with the litter picker in his hand.

"What do you reckon? Is he dead?"

"Well he ain't moving." Stig has a deadpan, emotionless way of communicating, particularly when you may be stating the obvious. I have a soft spot for Stig.

How ironic would it be to check out of this life in a flowerbed – already in situ for pushing up daisies. I offered to cross the platform as back-up assistance. Nobody wants to deal with a body first thing on a couple of sips of coffee. But first thing here means there is Stig and then there is me. Offering assistance is the neighbourly thing to do. I resist the temptation to suggest turning the litter picking claw into a cattle prod to determine dead or alive. Probably not in the Southeastern training manual.

Stig decided to call for official back-up. As he stepped away the body grunted. Drama over – daisies unfertilized – let the day recommence. *"Stig – Coffee?"*

I headed back into the coffee shop, just making it back behind the counter in time, as the first foot of the day stamped on the metal plate on its way in through the doorway. Open for business on time for the time-anxious London commuters who prefer the 06.05 – and the 06.13 at a push.

Chapter 2

Flat Broke – Regular

My MISDEMEANOURS HAVE been on an international scale – why limit yourself? I lived overseas on a couple of continents for several years – while wandering freely around others.

St Leonards-on-Sea was never on my radar. I had already discovered – from a stint on the Isle of Wight – seaside towns considerably narrow escape options unless you have an effective means of transport to escape by. Should you be a good swimmer – St Leonards is surprisingly close to France – alternatively – there are always the trains. I am still surprised to find myself here.

I moved to East Sussex from the Rock – (my nickname for the Isle of Wight) – with my partner of the moment – assuming optimism this time lay somewhere in the South Downs. It was the Rockies last time. I must have a thing for uplands. Whereas I understand the concept of home – I struggle with the definition. I always have done. Oxfordshire is the only county I have ever felt any real attachment to – although I have felt at home or made a home in many other locations. Some would argue too many – argue away. I cannot help having a love affair with the cardboard box. I get bored easily and love the thrill of a new adventure – I think the ratio is 30 moves in 25 years – and counting. What can I say – except that I am brazenly free spirited – or lost.

I irritatingly found myself stranded in East Sussex. It was an accident – I had not factored in every eventuality. When relationships break down – so do finances. I could not afford to return to my home county – so I had to make do with a temporary one – on the proviso that I would escape as soon as I could. The views from uplands are highly desirable for many, meaning unaffordable for me. I found myself at the bottom of my game, fairly near the first rung of the housing ladder – and not for the first time. This is how I, along with many others, arrived at St Leonards On Sea. Driven downwards by price. I could lie and say I wanted to live by the sea – or I heard it was the new Shoreditch – but it was my personal lack of attachment to the root of all evil. St Leonards – I know it sounds grand – it was once if you were Victorian. Its riches today are different – some of them cultural – some of them illegal – and to be quite honest – it's a bit of a shit-hole. But where there is shit there is the fertilizer known as opportunity. You just have to know how to find it.

Life was becoming frustrating. I pride myself on keeping my options open – yet I inadvertently found myself lost at sea, with no anchor, no flare and up to my neck in the proverbial mire. It is important to note that 'inadvertently' is just a polite way of saying 'fucked'. A long-term single mother recently made redundant from the most tedious of jobs just months after successfully battling to buy a house. Mortgages for single parents can be elusive.

Added to the misery was the sting of buckshot aimed at my flank. This flinch was inflicted on me by a psychopath. He was my protector. The only man I have ever met who would fight all my battles before I was even aware of their existence. He locked us both in a basement once – refusing to let me out until I told him how

I got the scars above my eye and back of the left thigh. Old scores were not his to settle. We were friends first and foremost – or so I thought – a rough, tough countryman to his core – proud to be a hunter and a gatherer. He taught me to shoot. He seemed to enjoy the art of killing and skinning. His knowledge of the great outdoor playground was vast and he could turn his hand to anything. He was once a bare-knuckle fighter – sparring for prize money because life had been hard to him. He lived in green moleskins and check shirts which missed the odd button. Psychopath could stop the hardest of men dead in their tracks with a glance – but would sit up all night to look after a sick animal – not of the hunted variety. It was only in hindsight I realised that I too was prey – hunted, stalked and captured. I had a lucky escape. I miss him – I know I shouldn't.

My odds were starting to stack up. I'm not great at percentages but a sinking feeling was giving me a fair idea.

Redundancy is typically a difficult time. It is a stinging slap in the face. A re-direction in the form of rejection. Any which way it's a loss. Losses should be seen as positive because they shape and grow a person. It can be hard to appreciate this when the bills keep landing on the mat. I hated the job anyway – business development for a pin-striped wanker – I was grateful for the shove – just not for the financial insecurity. I have to say I have worked for several pin-stripes in my time – the majority of whom have been wankers – perhaps there is a link to the pattern. Pumped to bursting point with their own self-importance – intimidating loudly to conceal their own weaknesses and piss poor management skills – whining and demanding I ply them endlessly with sustenance and an ego rub, dangerously balanced on a saucer – ready to dunk in the cup at their leisure – kicked back – at their desk – while blatantly hoping to shag me over said desk – because isn't that what I want? What we all want really? Let's think …. Erm … NO! You pathetic little wanker – which is all you will be doing – by yourself! Ask your wife maybe? I recall the second boss I had – ironically, he was named after a biscuit. He thought it would be exciting to dictate his sexual fantasy to me mingled seductively in amongst the board room minutes. My shorthand speed was fast – which made his fantasy … incredibly short-lived!

It is the minority pin stripes that left the deeper, lasting impression on me. Business men, sadly no women, with an acumen and instinct that I would have given my right arm for. I typically respect a minority.

It is often the creative risk takers like myself that lose their jobs. I am at my best when my back is against the wall – I think the word is adversity. No point behaving like a deer in a headlight – I always fight back. I was determined to turn my situation around. I decided to set up my own business, work for myself, and provide my three children with residential, financial and educational stability.

Coffee can be liquid gold. Captive markets are key for success so I investigated commercial opportunities at local stations. St Leonards was my nearest. The London-bound platform had a disused, uninspiring unit that required vision to highlight its potential (shit-hole). Strictly speaking it wasn't being advertised, but I persuaded the agent to meet me there. Relentless determination paid off in the form of a commercial lease.

Funding for a new business is a major hurdle because commercial lines of credit irritatingly require trading history. I found a local company specialising in start-ups, wrote a credible business plan and presented it enthusiastically to their panel. All I needed was £7,000 – it's nothing if you have it and everything if you don't. I convinced the panel I was risk worthy and drew down the funds. The lease was issued – my heart sank when I read Clause 10. Once upon a time, I studied law, believing naively that the subject was all about justice, before making the deflating discovery that law is just a game. The winner of this particular game is the player who manipulates the rules to their advantage while working within the parameters of legal constraint.

Although I did not pursue a career in law, I had learnt enough to recognise that Clause 10 could make me liable for the substantial repairs the unit needed. As the guarantor on the lease, this clause had the potential to bankrupt me. Superficially, the repairs looked like a paint job – in reality, they were structural – to the tune of thousands. Lease deposit already paid – I refused to complete on the lease until the work was done – nearly a year later. The delay was becoming a financial disaster as the loan repayments began with the drawdown. On completion, I only had a couple of thousand left to pay the contractor, purchase stock and equipment. I held my nerve, bought the opening stock on my personal credit card and flung open the coffee shop door. I am head strong and determined – failure is not an option – I have to be able to respect myself.

Never give up, never give up, never give up.

Lady Antebellum

'Good Morning – what can I get you?'
'Large latte – no the larger one.'
'Would you like a loyalty card?'
'Stamp one.'
'Good Morning – can I get a drink started for you as well?'
'No, I am not having that – I was first.'
'I know – I am just trying to get everybody served in time for this train.'
'I was still first.'

This insistence on priority status came from **Lady Antebellum.** A senior city high-flyer – slowly gliding downwards for a hard earned, cushioned landing – choosing to retire to St Leonard's – outrageous that she had to arrange her own retirement party.

She was my first female customer who went on to become a regular. She does not suffer fools, can be tricky and her bark can be worse than her bite – rather like myself. She bit me a couple of times – but I persevered – recognising that it was probably more to do with a process of self-establishment both sides of the counter. I respect her for her career stamina and her willingness to state her opinions in a forthright manner (basically criticise). If only she knew how much we had in common.

My first rap on the knuckles came when the coffee shop was in fledgling status. I was desperately trying to get everything right, learn my business and please everybody – all at the same time – on no sleep and no money.

I was in the process of serving her when a meeker, milder London form of pin stripe – a City banker – no, not a wanker – formed a very British queue. He was calm, patient and quietly accepting of the sixty second count-down till the train pulled in. This is when passengers typically realise the certainty of grabbing a drink for the journey becomes more of a lottery. I asked him if I could start a drink for him. Lady A was not amused. A tirade of telling off ensued and my defence system was instantly on high alert. Up went my back – I fought it down. *"Oh no – Oh no – I am not having that – I am old fashioned in that respect – I was here first."* Awkward. Lady A was right to be indignant. I wanted to be because I didn't deserve the admonishment. But this is where station coffee shop life has a different etiquette to that of the high street. The time constraint is obvious – everyone is rushing to catch the same train. The window of opportunity to get a coffee is a narrow one.

Because my machine is capable of knocking out four shots of espresso simultaneously, I do not see the harm in racking up the cups underneath and frothing enough milk so that everyone can have exactly what they want and catch the same train. A hot drink ensures a happy start to a tedious commute.

Prioritising the queue is a skill that I acquired quickly and quietly as I got to know my regulars. No need for a song and dance – I just know what they drink and prepare according to departure time. The need for coffee can make a person tetchy. Apparently, I am no different. I once had the misfortune to pull in to a Service Station on the M3. The elderly man in front of me reached for a sandwich from the chiller and promptly keeled over. I dropped to the floor, surrounded by misplaced false teeth and urine, his not mine, talking to 999 on my phone. As I tried to deal with the situation, people kept on stepping over us to retain their place in the queue. I was shocked by the number of heartless bastards travelling on the M3 that day. He died coffee-less – a travesty of justice.

Lady A has mellowed over time, as have I. Knowing each other a little better, she now appreciates I was trying to be accommodating rather than rude. Since her retirement she visits later in the day. She is always going somewhere – partial to the odd rock concert or two – as am I. Who knew – behind the boiled wool, Made in Britain, terribly smart black winter coat – there is a hell-for-leather rock chick trying to escape.

A younger me at times aspired to be like Lady A – powerful city player – promoted, respected and rewarded by status and trappings – the trophies of success in a corporate world and a money-driven society that I once bought in to wholeheartedly. I don't anymore. I am not just talking about money – of course we all need it. I like money because when the dull brown envelopes are paid, I don't need to worry about making ends meet in the middle of the night. In addition, whatever is left over can then be lavished on my free time collection of life experiences. But playing the corporate game – killing yourself in uncomfortable power suits, trussed up in tights to climb a ladder while avoiding snagging one – only to have your fingers trodden on as you reach for the top rung – working long hours to look good by being omnipresent – paying lip service over restaurant service – as the next bright young thing dims your light and years of effort and personal sacrifice are rewarded with an early dispatch to rapidly fading pasture – no – that game is not for me. A small life in the big City? Better a big life in a small town. My choice for now.

The transition from adolescent to adult is a tightrope – the height made me apprehensive. I avoided the shortcut and opted for the long way around – finding my own way. My career path changed direction frequently. I was a professional dilettante. I jumped from job to job – loving the challenge of something new before rapidly losing interest. I was terrified of being trapped in a dead-end job, stuck on repeat listening to the sound of monotony. Bored shitless by many an office, I looked desperately out of the windows, scanning the horizon for my next inevitable exit strategy. Turning my back on societal norms, but not on aspiration, I headed off into my own turbulent world in search of a greater unknown.

Whatever the measurement of success, it can only be achieved through a combination of hard work, determination and patience. I struggle with patience. I eventually studied law in my late twenties – eager to head down the long straight road of conformity in a world of black and navy – a private promise to make my dead Father proud. There is no room in law for a revolutionary – a former minority pinstripe and barrister told me this while trying to give me career advice. My inner rogue always ran away with me – hand in hand – dressed in our own hell for leather – we charged down different paths across the globe. I still like navy. We should all learn not to judge. The British public have a well-deserved reputation for being frosty, distant and difficult. But with time and familiarity we soften. If we relax a little, smile a little – the world inevitably becomes a far happier place – try it.

London bound, London proud, London bound, London proud.

As the trains roll on through I hear rhythm sounding out from the tracks. Track mantras gathering pace from the rails – messages for the journey. I like to tune in. My ear is musical, my hearing is sensitive. I diligently played the straight-laced piano and oboe from a young age while hankering for a dirty saxophone. This shiny brass carrot was dangled in front of me by my frustrated parents to 'encourage' me to study harder. It eludes me still.

"The train now approaching Platform 1 …"

One by one the commuters come, occasionally in pairs but never in groups. Long commutes are not pack activities. Commuters are a complex crowd with simple needs – coffee and efficiency. Some more bleary eyed than others, some with resignation not conversation. Some with attitude, some with none. The occasional hangover-on sea – inevitable if you know the Town's party calendar.

'Large vanilla latte – can I pay by card?'

Regulars can order simply by making an appearance or a 'polite' hand gesture. Insults to staff will not be tolerated. Recognition is acknowledgment of status. It is mutually beneficial, the epitome of excellent customer service, the foundation on which business success is built.

'Double espresso no lid?'

For those who didn't see the pavement sign – hurrying along the platform submerged in their phones – the coffee is Lavazza. Coffee too has purpose and status. It is the second most traded global commodity after petroleum – both fuels of a kind. Passengers **need** theirs. The tannoy drones on – roll calling the rush hour. As the morning trains rumble through – the pressure of commuting switches to my side of the counter. The queue builds up, commuters cram in wanting different coffees all 'to go' on the same train. None of us can afford to miss the connection.

Some of us make a connection, some of us make a statement, some of us make an impression. Hat tricks are rare – and some mornings are more extraordinary than others.

Cider With Rosie

A TRANSVESTITE DIVA in a shocking pink pencil skirt, tailored jacket, black crop top, abs to die for, fishnets, heels, designer handbag, and long black hair flounced into my coffee shop on route to his office. Flustered in a 'have I got news for you' kind of way – he plonked himself down on the pew – huffing and puffing – his heavy Gloucester accent becoming stronger as he vented into his mobile. The conversation ended abruptly – when the phone rang – he dinked the call.

I had a conversation with Stig about Rosie. He used to see him on the trains when he worked for Revenues. Rosie's real name was Tom. Tom objected to being thrown off a train for not having a ticket, shouting *"you can't throw me off the train – I am a lady!"* at the top of his voice.

Rosie adjusted his stockings and re-positioned himself on the pew – performance ready. Above the coffee machine hangs an invisible sign that invites customers to counselling with their coffee. I had no idea it was there – it must be customer facing. The customers chose to socially enhance me. With Rosie, the sessions began without warning.

The pew was an after-thought. I had seating reservations. Would anyone want to sit in and if they did, would I want them to if they didn't need to. The pew was a brilliant compromise – a customer suggestion. Just comfortable enough to perch on, no good for a nap, but a great place to begin an unburdening with a stranger. I just ask that you respect it – no shoes, no hot drinks on wood, no pets, no climbing. Just backsides, bags and briefcases please – and no outstaying your welcome.

What is the protocol when serving a man dressed as a woman who is most clearly a man? I decided to go with the flow and try not to cause politically incorrect offence. These circumstances rarely come with a rule book. There was no need to be gender specific anyway because in English, the latte is neither male or female – diversion into hot water outside the cup successfully avoided.

Rosie had to get the last 24 hours of distress off 'his' chest. All I had to do was listen. Customers came and went – giving him more than a cursory glance – or perhaps it was the eye – hard to tell. I will just say that he did a pencil skirt justice and I was slightly envious of his femininity. I love pink – but still feel guilty about possessing anything in the colour – I grew up understanding that the need for a colour was assessed by practicality – pink was nowhere to be seen. He made a beautiful woman – at least from the back. He had a figure he was proud of. Should body shapes actually be a measure of proudness? I think not. He reminded me of all the ridiculous feminine enemies I made or imagined during my younger years.

I did not trust women then. It has taken me a long time to fully understand the importance of female relationships in my life. Women can be bitchy, jealous and hostile to each other. Indirect aggression is a form of self-promotion. When a woman achieves the status known as success – it does not automatically follow that her own hand is extended to help other females along the same path. I think my conscious distrust in females began at primary school. Subconsciously, it probably began at birth. Little girls are not so much sugar and spice – more artificial sweetener. I am sure I was no different. Girls seem to struggle with friendship – two is company – three is a necessary crowd – because there always needs to be a scapegoat as they practice the art of skilful manipulation from a young age, alongside hopscotch and skipping ropes.

The importance of education was at the heart of my childhood and I was fortunate to be introduced to many different subjects. My love of music and drama was where my passion for the arts stopped. I never wanted to be a ballerina. The drawback of having a professional ballet dancer as a Grandmother meant that every bloody birthday another pair of ballet shoes would land on the mat. I was not one of those delicate little petals – more of a heifer really. I found ballet to be a discipline I could well do without – back to front cardigans with awkward ribbons, pastel shoes and litter trays to shuffle in. I did not want to dance – I still don't. The only pas de cheval I have ever been interested in is that of an actual horse. I was desperate to ride – and I did – as soon as I left home.

I declined the invitation to participate in all things girlie. I preferred to be one of the lads – opting for a very select handful of female friends with unsharpened claws. Lads were easy to hang out with – easy to dress with – no frivolity – jeans – t-shirt – biker jacket – bit of a swagger – a uniform I understood. I blended straight in.

I now realise I have missed out – or maybe women, myself included, are simply much better at friendships as we get older. I know I am. I have rectified the imbalance – but have still managed to retain my initial select handful. Genuine girlfriends will be there till the end – fake ones tend to show their true colours as they try to partner up with your ex. Boyfriends have a tendency to fall by the wayside, usually when they misread a road sign – or couldn't see it because someone has deliberately obscured it from view.

Rosie had been to the local pub the night before to have drinks with his boyfriend. He had been there twenty minutes when his no show boyfriend dumped him by text. Cowardly and ungentlemanly behaviour. I started to empathise. He assured me his night just got worse. Other drinkers began giving him abuse. He tried to fend them off but, realising he was up against it, decided to leg it. They chased him and punched him for dressing as a woman.

Preferring not to comment on the dress aspect, I decided to head for the relatively safe territory of the punching. I felt he needed protecting and asked him if he had called the Police. He looked horrified. *"No Way"*, he statemented in his best Gloucester. He informed me that he is not a grass and would never do that to someone in his local community. Misplaced loyalty? Rosie then went on to explain his personal outlook on life. He lives his life according to a mathematical formula based around percentages. He sees every part of everyday as a percentage of good and bad and cross-references (not dresses) that back to his own system of odds – I am most definitely following him now! He calculates that life experiences are based on percentages – some of them good – some of them bad. The odds are stacked so that not everything in one day can all be bad. When something bad does happen – he only allows a certain percentage to be allocated to that event. That way he always knows there is room for something happy in his day. Brilliant. Rosie was stronger than I gave him credit for.

I admired him for his guts to wear pink with such dramatic effect. Embracing all things female – proud to be girly. Flaunting sparkles and lipstick – designer and charity – accessorized and accentuated. Not intimidated by his own sexuality or the attitudes of others. Brazen in his self-acceptance. His game face was on for the world to see. I used to be more like him – *not* a transvestite – but more feminine – more social butterfly than sea-side hermit. The life of a young, carefree woman, with no responsibility and no one depending on her, is a self-indulgent one. I spent much of this time in Henley-On-Thames, sharpening my own knowledge of feminine wile as I flirted with the fringes of wealth and social status. I indulged on this open road of opportunity before packing up my life for one overseas in search of a more genuine community. Another societal pivot executed to perfection. In time, life changes all of us. High pressured jobs are overrated, high powered boyfriends are disappointing and tights are simply irritating. My femininity became buried as my ever-changing life demanded practical. Flats replaced heels. Sequined clutch bags replaced with a whole new baggage allowance. Denim – my wardrobe staple – replaced everything else. A statement of hard work and disobedience rather than fashion.

'Could you tell me where the toilets are?'
'No toilets at the station – sorry.'
'Can I help?'
'Large tea – bag in.'
'Is there really no toilet?'
'Sorry – no.'

Chapter 3

St Leonard of St Leonards-on-Sea

THE PATRON SAINT of pregnant women, horses and all those deprived of their freedom – both physically and mentally. Interesting! I presume this is who the town is named after. I am sure I am not the only one to wonder how they found themselves here. But it does have a charm all of its own. I reluctantly have to admit it may be growing on me.

When you open a business door to the general public you have no idea who will come through it. St Leonards and Hastings at the line's end have a deserved reputation for being a bit lively – not always in a good way. It's trying hard to shake off its image as a dumping ground for the mentally ill and a hunting ground for the drug driven. As a precautionary measure, I ensured the coffee shop counter was built higher than normal.

The Station, and my coffee shop, sit in the heart of St Leonards at the top of the Kings Road – the runway from the Station down towards the sea. As I begin to know the people, I have more affection for the town. When I first walked down this road with my blinkers on, most of the shop units were empty and the seagulls had strewn rubbish all over the streets. A ghost town. The once architecturally elegant commercial properties were bowed and forlorn, yet they still retained their beauty. Some retain their impressive doors and windows – a legacy from a bygone era. Charity shops and Bookies were in the majority. Hoodies hunted in packs without purpose, rough sleepers detracted from the beauty of a Georgian doorway. Mid-day domestics spilt out of pubs – their shouting contests drowning out the cries from lazy seagulls electing not to fish.

Over time, change becomes inevitable. St Leonards refuses to stagnate and decline. The coffee shop itself is evidence of the change. St Leonards is a closet commuter town. The controversial dividends of re-gentrification are starting to show, because gentrification does not automatically bring unity. For some, a John Lewis delivery van sighting in the area affirms their belief that property prices are on the up – to others they are as unwelcome as the Normans in 1066.

St Leonards on Sea – the Town for Me, St Leonards on Sea – the Town for Me.

Pronouncement

"This is a safety announcement. It is not permitted to cycle, skateboard or rollerblade within the station building."

PASSENGERS ALWAYS SEEM surprised by this announcement. A terribly unfortunate mobility scooter incident somewhere down the line is living testament, well actually dead testament, to the fact that if you inadvertently (fucked it), hit the wrong pedal or lose control of your mind or your wheels, you run a clear and present danger of flinging yourself head first to fry on the live rail. Listen to the tannoy as it preaches indifferently around the platforms, you know it makes sense. Delays, disruptions, cancellations, health, safety, weather, and cryptic advanced warnings. Passengers have mixed reactions to the announcements. Anything from irritation, frustration, outrage, laughter, genuine disbelief or anger. I am the buffer on which they vent. I am learning to filter unwelcome noise while adopting a sympathetic expression.

'Morning Steve – how are you? Usual?'
'All good – busy weekend – should've been a plumber not a copper – I'm knackered.'
'Extra shot then – should get you through.'

Steve catches blue (Southeastern) and green (Southern) trains with no fixed pattern. He serves the public in a different way.

Shrink into Significance

I WATCHED HIM catch his train and made myself an americano. I was beginning to wonder whether the coffee shop was at risk of becoming some kind of wellness lounge for travellers – free therapy session with every purchase – an interesting take on the meal deal concept. There are some who use the shop to condense and recount whole chapters of their lives in the time it takes me to make their coffee. I am astounded as to how much information some people can impart in a couple of minutes – some of which is very personal – before they mentally re-group – adopt a faceless expression and step out to get lost in the throng of platform anonymity afforded to strangers in public. They remain anonymous until their journey ends and they are catapulted back into character. The coffee shop is different – somewhere between the door and the counter, the aroma and the hiss, the exchange and the counsel – we make a connection.

Every day is as individual as every customer, but a distinctive recurring pattern was starting to form. As I prepare their orders, customers feel free to offload, comment, reflect, despair, laugh, share, question, ask, hide, reveal, educate, complain, cry – then depart. Not so much a wellness lounge – more a kitchen counselling counter – over which drinks and snacks are served.

It is important, from a customer service perspective, that I adapt to every situation. I listen – or pretend to depending if they are boring the arse off me – advise, sympathise or empathise. I silently count my own blessings – or voice theirs for them. Sometimes I laugh, or feel like crying – because of what they are saying or because they will not leave and I need a comfort break. Once behind the counter I am relatively trapped. I try to be sensitive and reserve judgement because judgement typically cultivates defensiveness. A defensive nature stems from insignificance. Sensitivity is the lighter approach to take. To achieve this realistically and empathetically, I have to pay careful attention to detail, while keeping the queue moving. We should all try harder not to judge – myself included – because it's easier to make snap judgments about people rather than give our time freely – consciously making the effort to help those who need to heal – even though their wounds may be cleverly concealed. I acknowledge the trust placed in me by complete strangers as they chat. On a personal level, trust is a concept I struggle with.

Despite my sometimes-abrasive exterior, (stop smiling if you know me personally), I am a compassionate being. I am generally happy to help someone – piss takers excluded. People may forget what you say, but they never forget how you made them feel – a mildly irritating statement – because sometimes if they remembered what I said, they might actually feel better. Some things I am told are shocking, some heart-breaking, some hilarious. Frequently my preconceptions are turned upside down. Rock-a-nory Ron is a perfect example. A former drug dealer and addict – I used to be very wary of him – he comes in on his way to work at a rehabilitation charity. Having turned his own life around, he now helps teenage drug addicts and gang members live a different life. He was someone who I would never have engaged in conversation in a former life. Someone who taught me a valuable lesson in dependency – when I needed him to find out information about a lowlife who was threatening the safety of a family member – his aftershave always lingered.

Proud Rebellion

STIG IS THE first person I ever spoke to at St Leonards. I appeared at his ticket office window to ask him for the keys to access the unit. I needed to measure up for the fit out. He sat there with his shaved head, steely expression, rebellious glint and invisible tattoos of hate and love. I smiled inwardly – something about his whole demeanour sparked memories of my misspent youth. Is there any other way to spend it?

I was a delightful young child – all hairbands and compliance. Somewhere around my teenage years – I became a complete arsehole – the paragon of rebellious. Rebellion – such a satisfying word to physically say as it rolls easily along the tongue – making a huge statement of independence guaranteed to cause intense confrontation with parents and authority as it does so.

Growing up, I had no fixed end destination in mind. No doubt too busy championing a rebellion somewhere. I once told my father I wanted to become a QC. His response being I wasn't academic enough. Not sure if he meant studious enough or bright enough. As my headmaster and parent, I concede he was well positioned to form an educated opinion. Either way it was both an exclusion and a rejection. Instead of proving him wrong, which is what I would do now, I redirected myself.

I bolted headlong into a world of heavy bikers, loud metal, red Marlboro and black leather – giving compliance and conformity a cheery wave goodbye with my right hand while raising the middle finger on my left. Fuck you then – and fuck me.

Motorbikes – I love them – they are so throaty – a mechanical form of saxophone. To this day, if I hear the thump of a meaty motorbike, daring a red light to turn green, it does something to me. I can ride – I shouldn't. I love riding pillion. An interesting exception for someone who is reluctant to trust. Once you throw your leg over the seat, you have effectively thrown yourself at the mercy of the leathers in front of you. I also love the smell of bike leathers because for me they are a symbol of freedom. Strange that they make me feel that way because riding pillion means you are being controlled, dominated and bound by the decision made by the helmet in front of you. I cannot deny there is something incredibly sexy about riding as one unit. I suggest you experience it for yourself.

My biker chick days started at the age of 15. I began hanging out with a band of Hells Angel wannabees from Long Wittenham. This involved under-age drinking at the Machine Man Inn, fast and furious hurtles through the conceited villages of Oxfordshire, all complete with unnecessary unison revving inviting the tarmac to a race. That sound excites me. The Windsor Chapter of the Hells Angels and their passion for axe throwing, both at home and away in the New Forest, was well known. Rumours were rife about the sexual initiations required to be an Angel's angel. I weighed up the pros and cons of shagging some meatloaf on an emblazoned fuel tank backwards while travelling at great speed and decided it was not for me. I stayed with the Wittenham wannabees. Rival biker gangs clashed – usually after a Dumpy's Rusty Nuts gig – a depicting name for a shit band. I have ridden with various gangs in my time – bikers gave me a taste of belonging.

My wardrobe was tiny – just two favourite t-shirts – one said 'Triumph', a statement I still live by, while the other said 'Born to Live – Live to Ride' – a deep and meaningful biker statement! There was of course the compulsory twinset – biker leather with a denim cut-off emblazoned with meaningful patches and matching jeans. Jeans define the innocence of virgin bikers as I discovered one night on the 90 degrees bend coming out of Long Wittenham towards Didcot – an Oxfordshire shit-hole! The prick on whose bike I sat had not put the centre stand up properly. As we rode into the bend, the stand kissed the tarmac and flipped the bike over. I was last seen inadvertently (definitely fucked it) sliding down the road on my knees to a 'seconds away from disaster' halt under the wheels of an approaching car. I had a lucky escape. The ambulance men were very helpful. The denim from my jeans was sitting on my knee cap somewhere where my skin used to be – the ankle – incredibly dodgy.

I had time to reflect in the John Radcliffe Hospital. My parents had been contacted – oh joy. When I had mentioned to them that I was going for a bike ride, they presumed it would be on the bicycle they saw me cycle down the drive on. My father was silently furious because I had lied. My mother was usually pissed off with me for something and probably for good reason – that I could handle. But my father would not talk to me for days. My timing for sustaining a leg injury was poor as it was just before a family camping trip around Europe. I sensed an opportunity to get out of it – fat chance. Instead, my siblings had to endure my leg stretched out across them in the back of the car as we travelled around France. I was left alone most days for quiet contemplation about my misdemeanours in a vintage orange tent with a huge stack of books to read – none of which were educational. Collins cums before Cooper. The true punishment came from the silence.

My rebellion worsened – I kicked and screamed against authority – ran away a couple of times, got engaged once, got suspended a couple of times, got unengaged, got expelled once – the usual teenage bullshit. When teenagers hurt on the inside – it has to manifest on the outside. I would like to think I showed a greater level of understanding teenage angst to my own children – did I mention I struggle with patience? In all honesty, I didn't understand my teenage years until I reached my forties. My biker attire was ceremoniously burnt by my mother as part of a peace agreement permitting me to return to school and get my Baccalaureate. Conformity enforcement. Knowledge brings greater freedom. I have my memories.

My love of bikes lives on – the leather long since replaced by matching BMW Kevlar – posh biking for grown-ups – trading country bends for twisting mountain passes in the Alps and the Dolomites – Stelvio or otherwise. The gear may have changed – but the exhilaration and the adrenaline rushes are even more liberating – probably because my awareness of danger has heightened with age.

Perhaps my sideways grin is because I believe a rebellious nature to be a good thing. If you refuse to simply accept what is, you allow alternative options to rise to the surface by rejecting restrictive boundaries and accepting the possibility of the untried and the untested. I love to push a boundary.

When I first asked Stig for the keys – he stared blankly back at me – no idea what I was talking about. My first insight into inter-station communication. I also expected him to be incredibly unhelpful. He wasn't. I had made an unfair judgment on a misleading first impression just because he looked like a hard bastard. Shame on me.

He spent ages trying every single key he could find until he hit the jackpot. I am sure he had reservations about the need for a coffee shop on the platform. He kept them to himself as he headed back to open up his window to a string of abuse from the queue that had formed in front of it. He gets far more abuse from his queue than I do. Perhaps he is selling something people don't really want but have to have – whereas I sell something people don't have to have but really want.

The station ticket office and the coffee shop both have a disproportionate ratio of staff to customers – namely one member of staff per shift. If you could bear that ratio in mind, it may make you see customer-facing station life from a different perspective. I feel compelled to defend the station staff – and all station staff for that matter – who are ignored, abused, shouted at, spat at and generally disrespected. When you set foot in the Station and buy a ticket – if the ticket machine will let you because it is everybody's enemy and relies on good internet connection – you become a passenger and the Station has a degree of responsibility for you. The Staff will help you if you are reasonable enough to actually let them. Bad manners cost good will and arguing the toss will always slow down a queue.

The ticket office generally gets bad press over the coffee shop counter around 10.00 am – break time – when customers vent their frustration in the coffee shop about the ticket office never being open. It *is* open – just not during a break – or a shift change. In your defence and theirs, people do not realise how early station life begins. By 10.00 am we are a good 6 hours into our day and a break should be considered well deserved.

Over time I noticed Stig's smile, dead pan humour, his loyalty to Spurs and his devotion to his family. He rides around on a Vespa emblazoned with the Union Jack. Too young for the Mod/Rocker

Quadrophenia of Brighton – perhaps he yearns after an era gone by – who doesn't.

During the months of delays and unexpected building repairs that followed – he joked about whether the coffee shop would ever happen. I was seriously starting to wonder. His look of indifference, shot from piercing blue eyes, comes from years of dealing with the general public venting all their frustration and travel anxiety at him – making it personal while ignoring the person – a talent the general public excel at – whilst being incredibly vigilant of their own personal rights and grievances.

I remember the day when a platform performer in his own personal oblivion, staggered down to the coffee shop, drunk and still drinking, ranting and raving – and then urinated all over my bin inside the shop. Resigned and irritated, it was Stig who came to my rescue with his heavy-duty gloves, cleaning fluid and station diffuser. He had my back. Stig is an unsung station hero. Look beyond his uniform. If he likes you he will help you. I suggest you learn to like him.

Stig makes me sideways grin – because there he is in his smart Southeastern uniform – conforming at the window. But if you look into his eyes – you will see the glimmer of defiance highlighting his own life-story– backed up by his green Parka and British flag.

"This is a safety announcement. Due to today's wet weather, please take extra care whilst on the station. Surfaces may be slippery."

'Do you have any croissants left?'
'No, sorry.'
'Oh shame …'

We do really – I just hid them. I know which train she's on. She buys a croissant, eats noisily on the pew with her mouth open, then leaves behind a trail of croissant destruction that I have to rush round and clear up, when I need to be concentrating on serving the morning rush. When she leaves, out come the pastries again. I consider this my concession to corporate time management.

"The train now approaching Platform 1 is the 06.23 Southeastern service (blue train) to London Charing Cross calling at West St Leonards, Crowhurst, Battle, Robertsbridge, Etchingham, Stonegate, Wadhurst, Frant, Tunbridge Wells, High Brooms, Tonbridge, Hildenborough, Sevenoaks, Orpington, London Bridge, Waterloo East and London Charing Cross …"

Charing Cross sits at the junction of the Strand, Whitehall and Cockspur street, just south of Trafalgar Square in London. Charing takes its name from the Old English word 'cierring' – which refers to a bend in the River Thames. This site is recognised as the centre of London for measuring road distances. The Cross gives its name to a music hall, which used to lie beneath the arches of the railway station – and commuter temperament when faced with delays.

Chapter 4

Emerging Tribes

As a society, we like to feel part of a tribe – an extended social group with distinctive economic and cultural benefits. St Leonards has two new tribes. Those who are Down From London and are instantly recognisable because their clothes are different – their idea of dress-down being designer shorts and branded flip flops. They too were drawn here by low property prices – buying up stunning houses they had seen featured in rose-tinted seaside articles. They are no longer passing through – having sold up and priced themselves out of a return ticket – off peak or prime. The second tribe is smaller – its members cautiously kept one foot in an enclosed shoe. They came, they saw, they retreat – confiding quietly to me over the counter that they had made a mistake – they miss 'Town'. I respect their honesty – one thing I have learnt along the way is never be afraid to lose face – wallowing in misery is pointless. Surrender the white flag and head off on a new adventure.

I know then, as I hand them their cappuccino – because it's not quite 11 o'clock – that I won't see them again. They are heading back to their own kind. I am sorry to see them leave with their optimism in tatters – their venture to the end of the line was just too limiting. I understand because – like them – I find myself here struggling with limitation. I have to make it work for now – but I refuse to join a tribe.

Died in Your Arms Tonight

Though I didn't fully recognize him, he was vaguely familiar. I found myself nostalgically drawn to his 80's rocker look. He needed a large coffee and a sausage roll to help him get to the South of France for a gig. He was part of Cutting Crew – an Eighties English rock band. I know this because he had to tell me. The Eighties – my defining era. Everything to love for, everything to live for. In eternal love with my boyfriend at the time, carefree, optimistic ambitious.

First love – the memories are sacred. Jon was different from the biker crowds I used to hang out with. Early twenties – tall, good looking, long blond hair – loved a rock band and a Ford Cortina – which we usually had sex in on the way back from the pub. I had good times with him – we went to Donnington Rock Festival in a Volvo – very rock and roll! We took off across Europe – inter-railing all over Scandinavia – camped among white reindeer at the arctic circle. Jon – I loved him – he was genuine, sexy, funny and reliable. I knew I could trust him implicitly – he was wrong to trust me.

I remembered Cutting Crew's greatest hit – released not long after my father died from leukaemia. I was 19. I was supposed to be at a party that night and had dressed accordingly – red leopard-skin trousers – ridiculously fluffy V-neck jumper – big 80's scrunched hair and thigh length, spikey, black suede boots – the look of a pretty woman – one I wore often. Teenage fashion – we've all done it. I remember what I was wearing so clearly – it was such inappropriate death bed attire – I counted the spots on my trousers as my father counted sheep for the very last time.

It was devastating watching him die in my mother's arms as his own lungs drowned him. Death did not become him. As the old song played in my head, I suddenly realised that I had been angry with him for dying ever since. In my heart, I know he stayed as long as he could. His death left me feeling abandoned and unprotected – probably until I met the Psychopath. I replaced his love with renewed distrust. His absence remains a void in my life. Learning to grieve meant I could not handle love.

I ruthlessly sabotaged my first love relationship with Ian. We worked together at the Barley Mow – Clifton Hampden – 6ft 6 with dark hair – gorgeous – long summer nights with Dire Straits – an appropriate title for our relationship. To this day – we should not be left alone in the same room. I last saw him on my 50th birthday – an inadvertent (fuck fest) private celebration of our 35-year connection at the Hotel Du Vin by a river.

Of course, I am sorry for the way I treated Jon – a devoted and supportive boyfriend – he deserved better. We remained in touch. Despite it all, he bought two one-way tickets to Australia and came to me with a question. Only one got used. I loved him – but I could not tell him – the words were in my head – where they remained. He left without me. Privately devastated on many levels – I went on the burn – leaving a trail of broken hearts belonging to those brave enough to die in my arms. Power ballads – who needs them. I got over it. I presume they did too – I never bothered to ask. Torn hearts heal with scar tissue that is invisible to the naked eye. Keep moving on. I have never needed a man to define me and solitude can actually be luxuriously selfish. I have a reluctancy to relinquish my personal space. Sex is easy – far easier than a long drawn out dinner which requires conversation to deflect uncomfortable silences. Love requires commitment. I remain non-committal.

The Importance of Earnest Belonging

Belonging is a basic human emotional need. It is the desire to belong to something greater than yourself and a need for reciprocation of attention from others. The sense of belonging to a community improves emotional and physical well-being for all those included – safe in the knowledge that they are not alone. To accept belonging also means accepting the concept that there must also be those who do not belong. Exclusion causes pain and conflict. Solitude fights against a basic need. Although belonging provides a safer haven – in order to belong you must conform to the restrictive rules of that community. The fight to resist conformity is mine. I choose to remain a rank outsider.

Attended Baggage

"Please do not leave your luggage unattended. Unattended luggage may be removed or destroyed by the security services."

This particular incident still makes me cringe with embarrassment. I made my enquiry innocently and the way it was taken could not have been further from the sentiment in which it was spoken, so I consider myself absolved. Enjoy a laugh at my expense.

A gentleman struggled into the coffee shop with two huge suitcases. He was exhausted just getting through the door – unaware of the hike he was about to embark on. His first problem – he needed a toilet – no public toilets at the Station. His second problem, a pre-booked ticket back to Norfolk and his train was not for another two hours. His third problem, his wife had got on an earlier train and left him to struggle back with two huge suitcases – chivalrous on his part – or a shrewd move on hers.

He asked politely if I could look after his suitcases for a couple of hours, which caused me to morph into some kind of top level security expert, saying in the interests of public safety I could not possibly guard his bags in case they contained a bomb.

Yes, yes, I really did say that – it just came out of my mouth – and although I could have possibly phrased it better – security is heightened everywhere and the Station has strict rules about unattended luggage. My coffee shop sits on a public platform. By default, I have a duty to uphold public safety. Toilet provisions are not in my remit. Anyway, imagine if there had been a bomb in his bag? The subsequent fall out would have been far reaching. The almighty explosion of the verbal variety was deafening. I had stepped on the racism landmine.

"Have you any idea how offensive that question is? Are you questioning me just because I look different? Because of my ethnic background?"

Cue the dramatic freeze framing, time standing still, wishing the floor would 'open up and swallow me whole' type of music – because those thoughts are genuinely not in my mind to cross. Time to disarm and work fast on my own charm offensive. I explained the reasoning behind my statement. Accepting my justification, he descended slowly from the ceiling and made his way back to the luggage.

Acute mortification for me then followed, as he felt the only appropriate course of action was to unpack the entire contents of both suitcases and lay them out in front of me: two sleeping bags, two air beds, a couple of pillows and a foot pump. Fortunately, it was not the Sunday morning shift, where these items may have potential street value for the Saturday nighters sleeping it off on the benches. He explained that he had sold his empty St Leonards apartment and had come down with his wife to finalise the details – hence the camping equipment. At this point I felt I had little choice but to agree to mind the bags. How could I refuse? We parted company as friends – all misunderstandings swept away under the sleeping bags. For me this remains the ultimate toilet drama. Nothing has come close – please do not consider that to be a challenge.

I reflected on this incident following a conversation with a local actor/film director/wine merchant (hyphenates are commonplace at St Leonards). He had acted in Trevor Griffiths' play – 'Oi for England' – the 80s was also the punk, skinhead, tartan, Stiff Little Fingers era and this play was an attempt to unite audiences against fascism. Why does history keep repeating itself? This play is ripe for revival.

Racism should not exist anywhere. I have experienced its mildest form twice in my lifetime. Once in China in the 90s – on a dodgy holiday with my old neighbour (long-standing female friend). We went on strange excursions out of Beijing where the locals laughed at us for having big noses – I think at the time I was relieved it was only my nose – as I was hanging on to a size 10 by a thread.

The second time was inconvenient. I found myself living in Okinawa for a couple of years – with my 'bipolar' American husband and three children under five. Okinawa is a turquoise and white subtropical gem with a history of occupation. The American military remains a huge presence there. Americans were not welcome everywhere. I tried to get a haircut. The shop sign said and meant Okinawan only – along with the buses – their doors shut in my face numerous times leaving me struggling home with groceries and pushchairs. Respecting their standpoint and their emotive occupation – I got a car.

"This is a security announcement ... " I rest my case.

'Hi Steve – large latte?'

'Oh yes – you alright?'

'No – I put my foot right in it yesterday … bomb … bag.'

Steve (the copper) put his head in his hands.

'Tell me you didn't say that to him – you can't say that to people.'

Calling the Shots – Regular or Large

THIS IS WHAT you do when you run your own business. I've lost count of the number of customers who told me they themselves had thought of opening a coffee shop here. *Only they didn't.* Such an easy thing to say as you get on the train to employment – where your pay cheque is guaranteed – same day every month – along with any other benefits you receive being employed.

I get a buzz every single time I unlock the door to my unit. I'm free from the constraints of a corporate straitjacket – no need to attend a meeting about a meeting – I just make up the rules as I go along. All huge positives. I sometimes give business advice to customers looking for their own escape – my advice is the always the same – if your dream doesn't scare you it's not big enough – minimise the risk wherever you can – then hold your nose and jump.

The drawback to all of this is working out how to afford free time to satisfy my need to roam, so I don't feel trapped by a brand-new straitjacket. Time off requires staff who have to be paid. I won my corporate freedom by being prepared to learn hands on while manning the front line. I took a huge risk working for myself and fought hard to make it happen – I must be careful to ensure one freedom does not overshadow another. I work too hard – regularly.

'Mate – I need a bloody off-peak return to Brighton.'
'Can't operate the stupid machine.'
'That's because the internet is down.'
'It's never working.'

Edward The Blue

EDWARD IS THE station elder – experienced, wise, kind and sensible –
he's mastered St Leonards Warrior Square. Once an entrepreneur and
innovator in his own right, he is an invaluable source of knowledge,
a believer in good manners and appreciates old school values. He is
another unsung station hero – always keeping a friendly eye out for
me and the coffee shop, in case I encounter any platform problems.
He uses patience and logical reasoning to disarm the disconcerted
and move the queue along. This ensures everybody stands a chance of
getting on the train with a ticket – even when the yellow jackets are
on the gate-line, randomly ticket-checking and slowing everything
down. These jackets belong to agency staff – some of whom are
passionately disinterested in the swift execution of any kind of ticket
check – but are always first in the queue at the coffee shop!

Edward and Stig are complementary opposites with the Station
in common. There is no hierarchy among the station staff – there
evidently is amongst the passengers. Self-importance is defined by
self-perception.

*"The train now approaching Platform 1 is the 06.31 Southeastern
service (blue train) to London Charing Cross calling at West St Leonards,
Crowhurst, Battle, Robertsbridge, Etchingham, Stonegate, Wadhurst,
Frant, Tunbridge Wells, High Brooms, Tonbridge, Hildenborough,
Sevenoaks, Orpington London Bridge and Waterloo East ..."*

Waterloo East is a central London railway station. It opened as Waterloo Junction in 1869, replacing Blackfriars Road station. It is mentioned in HG Well's novel 'The War of The Worlds' and is an indirect reference to toilets.

Cup Size – explain and discuss in no more than ten thousand words

'Regular or Large?'
'What is the difference?'
'4 oz. and a double shot.'
'What does 4 oz. look like?
'Smaller.'

Who knew cup size could become so controversial? This was an early mistake of mine which took the best part of a year to rectify. As a New Age nation of coffee drinkers, we have become obsessed with cup size and lost sight of what is after all the most important ingredient of the 'latte' – the strength and quality of the coffee. We fell for size over quality. How greedy and ignorant. High street chains started serving coffee and calories in buckets, the lifting of which required good bicep definition (I get mine from the morning milk run). A very long way from the elegance surrounding the European delivery of a latte or cortado – where it is, and always will be, all about presenting a coffee at its best.

My initial thought was to make the regular 8 oz. and the large 12 oz. However, having seen my competitors' cup sizes, I felt obligated to compete. Big mistake. Instead of going with my gut feeling, (Italy, and all the research and development done by Lavazza), I decided to change the cup sizes for 12 oz. and 16 oz. This suited many but displeased many more, because the coffee shot was being excessively diluted with milk and no longer provided the requisite hit.

After much consideration, I reverted to the original sizes, and had to face considerable outcry from hard core, caffeinated regulars who felt volume deprived – and despite lengthy discussions – were not happy with the smaller size or convinced by my explanation of quality versus quantity. Yes, you could simply put another double shot in the giant cups – but do you want to pay extra for it? This then makes them quadruples and their drinkers run the risk of doing star jumps on their morning commute.

When faced with a problem I will always find a solution – and as loyalty is worthy of loyalty – I continue to keep a special stock of cups just for my 16oz. lovers. I recognise the importance of diversity and customer satisfaction. They are a minority group who will eventually phase themselves across to the majority – but I will support them while they transition.

Put A Plaster on It

'S'cuse me – got any wet tissues?'
'Why do you need them?'
'I fell off my bike on my way here and my leg is bleeding.'
'Here – blue roll and napkins – are you ok? Would you like a plaster?'
'Nah – you're alright. If I go into work and milk this I will get a good half hour off my shift.'

Off she went as I inwardly thought I would never employ her with that attitude. The coffee shop has a first aid kit and administers basic first aid in various forms. Rushing for a train can be risky – pavements are lethal on wet days – as is the booking hall floor

– despite the bright yellow warning triangles – people still skid on through as they forget to look up.

I have a lovely, cheerful, warm-talking Scottish regular. She is always smiling. She could be acting but I think she is genuine. I do love Scotland. It's people are patriotic and they are always proud to form a tribe. She is a drama teacher in London during the week and suffers a different drama on Saturdays – inflicted on her by the 'So Tunbridge Wells' set at a boutique hairdresser's – a set with their heads so far up their own backsides that the job must be physically impossible.

These are exactly the sort of women I have never aspired to be like. I have avoided them like the plague because everything about them is false. Their mannerisms and seemingly effortless self-presentation at the salon is, in fact, all carefully orchestrated to reflect their social aspirations – and to ensure one-upmanship over the woman sitting in the salon chair next to them.

Although their personas are cleverly cloaked in foils – they remain transparent. They have given up sugar, carbs, snacks, meat – in fact – they are nil by mouth – including penis. They spend hours talking pretentious shit – having called their children equally pretentious names – deliberately designed to make it harder for their imported nannies to pronounce. It is, after all, far easier to dump your children off with a nanny – the fat, ugly one – code word 'safe' – that they chose specifically for their looks and child care abilities. They feel reassured, safe in the knowledge that their sex starved husbands won't be attracted to this kind of nanny, nor will they be tempted to shag said nanny in the nursery. Oh – except they did – because in some men's worlds – a fat, ugly woman is such a grateful shag. This is according to a conversation I once had with a pinstripe bragging about his extra-marital dalliances – wanker.

Foils and infidelity will probably end up divorced – but not until Foils has calculated her financial entitlement and retained a dear solicitor to secure her a small fortune and ensure pretentious status remains intact. Beware the flash of her perfect white smile and glinting highlights as she sits in the salon sipping a glass of bubbles, pouring over Tattler magazine with one ear to the gossip grapevine in oh so Royal Tunbridge Wells. I wouldn't cut their hair for all the coffee in Costa Rica!

Scotland hobbled in one morning visibly shaken and sat on the pew – bicycle tarmac incident – a huge round bleeding hole on her knee cap where the denim used to be. Remembering how painful that can be, I crossed the counter line and helped her put a plaster on the wound – which stuck out like a proverbial sore thumb. Catering plasters are blue in case they fall off in your food – they are easier to locate. I felt for her – bad start to the day – shaken, sore and late.

As she left I reflected on the pros and cons of plasters. At the time, you are grateful for one – slap it on over the injury – and away you go. Over time, they wear and fester until you forcibly have to rip them off as they hang on to your skin for dear life – desperate to conceal the truth underneath. 'Let the air get to it – it will heal quicker' – my advice to everyone but myself.

I have put a few plasters on my own life. I am always quick to fix the symptom but not the root cause. Roots are meant to be buried. It is incredibly difficult to take a long hard look at yourself and realise that you are not perfect when you consider yourself to be a perfectionist.

I think I have always struggled with conformity. It first became evident as a Headmaster's daughter. The very fact that I had a label meant I stood out from the crowd – teenagers prefer to be unobtrusive within their own hierarchy. It didn't help that the school I went to was relatively small – rammed to the rafters with the offspring of exceptional European Scientists who had inherited their parent's genes. I was expected to be intelligent – I suppose I am – unless its Maths or Physics. My mind does not work that way. I remember listening incredulously to the teacher ask me to work out how long it would take to fill up a bath with the plug out and the taps running – what would be the fucking point of that – just put the plug in. The lengthy detention did not alter my view. They never did.

I found myself frequently in detention for various crimes – some I committed – some I did not – some I never got busted for – like this one. The school was a gothic style, 19th century building in the middle of nowhere with a dark, spooky basement – we lived in a house in the grounds. I mischievously acquired the keys from my Father's coat pocket and organised a drunken rave – fifty of us partied undiscovered until dawn.

It is always good sport to drop a headmaster's daughter in the shit if you can – particularly one with a track record. My crimes were fairly routine – usually smoking behind the chapel – or not paying attention in class. Occasionally they were worse – like the time I had a physical altercation with a fellow pupil – he deserved it for trying to associate me with a shoplifting offence he had committed himself. It would have been physically impossible for me to commit the offence as I was grounded as usual. Still, violence is no excuse whoever you are and I was duly sent to the Headmaster's office. He expelled me on the spot. What choice did he have? It made for a very frosty dinner at home that evening.

That was the second time I ran away. The first didn't count. I spent a night on the school roof before slinking in through the back door, tired and hungry. At the time, the 390 bus to freedom and

London stopped at the top of the road. I jumped on it and ran away to Croydon. Who in their right mind runs away to Croydon? My Father coaxed me to return several months later for re-admission to school. I managed to behave during lessons. I believe that's known as meeting someone half way. I am glad I did – because my Father was ill – he had been for several years – I just didn't fully understand the implications of his illness. 'When teenagers hurt on the inside – it has to manifest on the outside' – it can take a life-time to understand the cause. I cannot change the past – but now I am a parent – I have a level of regret for the embarrassment I must have caused him in his own workplace. To his credit – he never gave up on me – patience of the proverbial saint.

My stand against conformity continued for many years – it probably still does – but I have responsibilities that demand I comply – namely motherhood – and I will comply because I take my responsibilities very seriously and honour my commitments. I respect that my actions will invariably have consequences for my children.

'What would you like?'
'Latte and a cappuccino with chocolate.'
'Toilet?'
'No, sorry.'

I have to keep the cold milk, chocolate and cinnamon my side of the counter – originally, they were self-serve next to the sugars – but self-serve got confused with self-help.

"The train now approaching platform 1 is the 06.40 Southern service (green train) to Brighton calling at Bexhill ... "

Bexhill is not, despite its reputation, where old people go to retire because it is steep in places – although it does smell of wee sometimes depending on the direction of the wind. It proudly hosts the Grade One listed De La Warr Pavilion on the seafront. St Leonards too has its own iconic building on the seafront – the landlocked ocean liner that is Marine Court – its foundation stone ironically laid by the Chairman of Southern Rail in 1936.

Chapter 5

Bo Peep Tunnel

CUT INTO THE hillside at the end of Platform 1. The tunnel and the nursery rhyme take their name from smuggling history – the action of 'looking out' from the cliffs – done by both perpetrator and law enforcement. St Leonards is successfully shaking off some of its more negative connotations – let us try to assume that it is no longer contraband central. Bo Peep's sheep seem to surround me. I am not entirely sure why. This is not meant in a patronizing way. It could be because I prefer to lead – or they prefer to be led – until their own path becomes obvious.

The tunnel – a wide dark mouth into which the trains disappear, transporting and transforming commuters away from laid back beach combers to city slickers fighting for survival in pressurized environments full of targets, obligations, time constraints, expectation, achievement, disappointment and exhaustion.

When I hear people complain about commuting, I just give them their coffee with a smile. Freedom is a choice – be brave enough to risk it. You will become both poorer and richer.

Little Bo Beep has lost her sheep; Little Bo Beep she cannot speak.

Ticket Out of Your Comfort Zone

'How fast can you make me a coffee?'
'Fast – what would you like?'
'Quick – my train is coming.'
'What would you like?'
'Oh – er – I don't know – a coffee of some kind – maybe a latte – no americano – no – maybe – oh no my train is here!'

The average journey time between London Charing Cross and St Leonards is 1 hr 36 minutes – with 24 chances on an average weekday. Customers seem to love a game of chance. If you are standing on the London bound platform – even though the tannoy announces the arrival of the train – it still has 90 seconds to come through the Hastings tunnel – stopping literally outside my coffee shop. You want a coffee and decide to chance it. You have got time provided you don't dither between the counter and the door – then the door and the counter – and back again. You panic – shouting *"I don't know if I have got time – can you make it quick enough?"* over and over – failing to actually order. This game drives me to distraction – I have already mentioned I am not a last-minute sort of person.

Let me share this handy hint with you – if you shout your order from the doorway, you get a coffee and make your train – I get a sale. A win-win. If you prevaricate and deliberate, angsting and stressing – incapable of making any decision – then it becomes a lose-win. You lose because you get to travel all the way to London without a coffee, or you lose because you manage to miss your train, even though it is right there in front of you. I then have to try not to find this amusing. I win because invariably you will still buy a coffee and sometimes more snacks, as you have at least a half hour wait on the platform. The downside to my win is that I then have to listen to you complain, (possibly sitting on the pew talking while eating), about how you missed your train – which could all have been avoided with a moment of decision-making – and I then get to regret suppressing my earlier amusement.

Something strange takes over passengers when they are about to travel. They behave more irrationally – anxious about the journey ahead – forced out of their comfort zone – forced in to sharing carriages with strangers. Excessive eating and drinking behaviour has long been recognised as a coping mechanism. This is clearly substantiated in the coffee shop. Small waves of panic buying – grabbing snacks and drinks – just in case. Obviously, this is good for business. Attitudes to others and tolerance levels change as unnerved passengers jostle for pole position on the platform – desperate to alight the train first – ignoring the fact that you need to let people off the train before you can get on it. The first prize for pole position is the chance to drape everything over a table for four – trying to make it look as if the seats are 'already taken' by a travel companion – probably locked in the ever mal-functioning toilet.

The second prize – a double seated opportunity – one for them and the other for their incredibly important bag, designer or otherwise, which must rest in comfort on the aisle seat while impersonating a passenger. This affords them the luxury of retaining their anonymity as they curl nonchalantly into the window. Both prize winners spend the entire onward journey panicking at every stop that a new passenger will be brave enough to ask them to move themselves or their belongings.

'Quick – large black.'

I look out for the alternative commuter in the rainbow bobble hat with turquoise pompom and year-round shorts. He jumped on his train with a coffee one day right after I realised his shots had misfired. This would have made his coffee too weak. I waited a couple of days for him to come back in. He didn't. I wouldn't have done either. I saw him one morning from the doorway and went to find him coffee-less on the platform. I handed him a free, leaded, large black americano as an apology. He now comes in every day – late. His train is always busy – I usually see him out of the corner of my eye while processing the queue. I quietly fit his coffee in amongst the others. We both appreciate his regular status and disrespect for any kind of time management. I laugh when he shouts *"I fucking love you"* from the doorway as yet again he just makes his train – clutching his large black like an Olympic torch.

"The train now approaching Platform 1 is the 07.06 Southeastern service (blue train) to London Charing Cross calling at West St Leonards, Crowhurst, Battle, Robertsbridge, Etchingham, Stonegate, Wadhurst, Frant, Tunbridge Wells, High Brooms, Tonbridge, Hildenborough, Sevenoaks, and London Bridge …"

King William 1 rebuilt London Bridge following the Norman Conquest in 1066. The current London Bridge was designed by architect Lord Holford and opened by Queen Elizabeth II on 17 March 1973. St Leonards is geographically removed yet physically connected. Bridges are built to facilitate communication. When London Bridge was attacked, a sea of strangers morphed into a community to support its recovery. The coffee shop is also a place where bridges are built.

London Bridge is falling down, falling down, falling down. London Bridge is resolute.

Constant Objection

THE COFFEE SHOP counter is a stage with performers either side – we endeavour to play our part to the best of our ability and not forget our lines (or improvise with others). Sales of any kind is basically acting. But if you sell with sincerity, customers are likely to feel valued and more inclined to return. There are those whose main objective is to complain about everything, living off self-created drama. Others create a box set all on their own.

Harriet Harpie – comes in fairly frequently – dark straggly bob – early thirties – two feral children who leap about on the pew, take stock off the counter and out of the chiller while she ignores them. She is irritated and tutting on arrival and departure. She wants a coffee. I have learnt that it doesn't matter which particular coffee because I can guarantee that it will be wrong for her. Harriet is a chronic complainer trapped in a negative reality which gives her even more to complain about. Complaining is a thought pattern. The more you complain, the more you effectively order more of the same for yourself, as you dwell on negativity. The way a customer complains says as much about them as the coffee they order.

When I complain – I vent. I have a threshold of tolerance and when something pushes me over it – I unleash. Venting is not healthy. It is a subconscious way of soliciting attention through anger and frustration and solves very little. The coffee shop has taught me that this is not a great attribute and sometimes you just have to let things go. I am working on it and now actively seek to comment on positives rather than just roaring about negatives – it's a process. Being on the receiving end of the unpredictable general public exposes me to complainers who bring everyone's mood down. It is not the complaint that people remember – it is the way that complaint was delivered – and how it makes the recipient feel! Effective complaining should be instrumental and infrequent. I am learning that this is a much happier way to achieve dispute resolution – for which my children are grateful – at home and in public.

Complaining clearly makes Harriet Harpie feel self-important and good about herself. She will never be satisfied. I will entertain the charade for now. Her defensive edge is off-putting. She needs to work on her charm offensive. Like I said, she is not the only one.

Tatz – Saturday Staff

STAFF ARE A luxury most small start-ups cannot afford. I got used to working some very long months because of this. Fortunately, family are not staff, they are volunteers. Tatz – my stoic, supportive, loyal, stubborn, amusing and insightful teenage daughter, was the coffee shop's first recruit – whether she wanted to be or not. Her positivity and unfaltering belief that all my ideas are good and that I will succeed at everything, made me even more determined to prove her right. It is important to be a good role model. Children do not want to see their parents fail.

Tatz was on hand during those early months, always optimistic and encouraging – the child parenting the parent – as we experimented with what worked and what didn't. The silent but deadly eye roll if I snapped in a stressed, motherly kind of way behind the scenes. The employer/employee parent/child waters got a little muddied at times. Although Tatz is young, her insight can sometimes stop me in my tracks. During a particularly stressful period in my life, she once left me a note that said simply – 'If things don't go right – go left' (with a few flower doodles to cheer me up). I frequently go left.

Tatz and the coffee shop have a mutually beneficial relationship. She has helped the business succeed, and in return, the business has given her the mixed bag of work-life experience that you can only gain from serving the general public in real time. This includes confidence, transport knowledge, more tolerance, an eye for dodgy characters, and the first and most important rule when running a small business – whatever the situation – you have to deal with it. It's called maturity.

Shoplifters are an occupational hazard – most are easily identified and barked off the premises. My Father gave me an early primary age lesson in thou shalt not steal. The fact that I still remember it proves its effectiveness. It was Christmas time in a florist near Winchester, I presume we were picking up a gift for my grandparents. Florists are tedious shops for young children and they smell mouldy. I saw a tiny Christmas gnome with a swinging lantern in a flower pot at my hand level. It was love at first sight and I slipped him in my pocket. Once back at the car, I was too excited to leave him hidden away and retrieved him back into view … *"look what the lady gave me…"* My Father always had a nose for bullshit. He took me straight back to the shop to apologise. I remember the lady – she said I was welcome to keep him. I left with an empty pocket and returned home under a very dark cloud. I now despise gnomes and dank smelling buildings.

Shoplifters try to target Tatz's shift. Be warned. She is eagle-eyed and easily affronted. I was out of sight behind the chiller one day when a reasonably respectable-looking woman came in and asked how much the pastries were – before stealing a bottle of water from the chiller. I can interpret frantic hand gestures, particularly when they are Tatz's. Cheek of the woman. There are those in the town who are desperate. However, if you are on a blue commuter train you are affording to go to work (unless you are chancing your arm with Revenue), you are therefore stealing through greed not need.

Irritated, I went out on to the platform, watched her grab a free (obviously) Metro newspaper – before heading back down the platform – engrossed in texting on her expensive smartphone. I stood in her path till she collided with me.

"That water in your pocket – today I will let you have it – because I'm feeling generous"– I growled at her.

She paled visibly. So did Tatz behind the counter because I am tall with a big personality, fluctuating frame size and little fear. Do not steal from me. I don't suffer fools or low life and am willing to break up a street brawl if I have to. Best not to push me.

It's the principle – I will go to my grave on one. In St Leonards, the shoplifter's need is usually 'coke' related. It is not the cost of the bottle that is so relevant – although if everybody just stole anything then of course it would be relevant. It is the principle behind it – and the one in front of it – and the one to the side of it. If you are the one that takes the risk, that works relentlessly on the business, in the business or for the business, if you lose pillow time, family time, play time, and me time – because it is more important to drive something forward, to sustain it and grow it and strive to make a better life for your family – then the principle is everything. These days my fuse is much longer – I believe that is also known as maturity.

Get a life low life, get a life low life, Get a life low life,
And stay out of mine, low life.

"The train now approaching Platform 1 is the 07.28 Southeastern service (blue train) to London Charing Cross calling at West St Leonards, Crowhurst, Battle, Robertsbridge, Etchingham, Stonegate, Wadhurst, Frant, Tunbridge Wells, High Brooms, Tonbridge, Hildenborough, Sevenoaks, and Orpington ..."

Orpington was a quiet country village set in the heart of fruit farms and hop fields until the railway came. It's parish church pre-dates the Doomsday Book. An Orpington is also a breed of chicken – in the buff or otherwise.

Three Strikes and You are Out

IF ONLY THAT were the case. For anyone lucky enough to be out of the country for a couple of years and far from the madding crowds of disgruntled Southern rail passengers – here is the briefest of accounts – because it was so incredibly boring.

St Leonards Warrior Square is a Southeastern Station (blue trains) but also has Southern (green) trains to Brighton and London Victoria. For some reason, the blue trains feel superior to the green trains – perhaps blue is a better colour for business – more metropolitan. Green represents nature and envy – harmony and growth – and has (ironically) strong associations with 'safety'. The green trains just seem more provincial. Possibly because not all green trains are empowered to go to Gatwick or Victoria.

These lesser green trains chug slowly through the scenic Sussex countryside, parallel to the South Downs, laboriously shuttling passengers between St Leonards and Brighton – probably wishing they were blue trains. To use them regularly is an exercise in patience.

When the coffee shop opened, the Southern Strike was in full swing and impacted every business reliant on railway users, including mine. On strike days, my takings halved. The strikes and the Southeastern engineering works were a miserable combination making tough conditions for everyone. I run a small business with narrow margins and no compensation for rent on strike days. Tied in to a commercial lease with my family's security on the line, I needed the trains to run according to the timetable.

The strike gripe – door operation and removing conductors from the train – the consequence – RMT called strike after strike – succeeding in causing severe disruption and damage to my customers' lives – because they couldn't get to their chemotherapy treatment; they lost their jobs because they couldn't get to work time and time again; they missed their college exams because students do not have enough money to get a taxi all the way to Brighton or London. The opening and closing of a door so far down my customers' priority list on the one hand – and so at the top of it on the other.

Replacement buses – implemented for engineering works and strike days – the scourge of the train passenger but particularly for those at St Leonards – because nobody ever quite knows where they go from. An occasional driver has braved coming up the Kings Road to the station – a jackpot moment if you are dragging heavy luggage. The official bus-stop location is as convenient as the public toilet situation. It is right down on the seafront – which from the station is a brisk fifteen-minute walk – at least it is downhill.

"Here is a special announcement. A replacement bus service is in operation ... "

Impossible to hear the rest as the language turns the air as blue as the Southeastern logo.

Nobody cares, nobody cares, nobody cares ....

"The train now approaching platform 1 is the 09.09 Southern service (green train) to Brighton calling at Bexhill, Collington, Cooden Beach, Normans Bay ... "

Norman's Bay is a coastal hamlet found among the Pevensey Levels. This Victorian station was built for the Londoners who flocked to see a whale stranded in the marshes (these marshes are now much further out to sea). Today – beached whale sightings are probably human.

Lights, Camera, Action!

'Got any cold drinks?'
'All there in the chiller.'
'What about energy drinks?'
'Coffee?'
'Yes, large flat white, muffins … everyone grab muffins, crisps and chocolate bars.'

It had been a busy morning requiring a mid-shift trek to the station bins. On my way there, I was blasted with the sickly smell of weed, being blatantly smoked right outside the Station by some pasty-faced grime in a grey hoody with sagging, dirty tracksuit bottoms. St Leonards version of street performer. On my way back from the bins, I walked past a mother sitting on a station bench, grooming through her daughter's hair, picking out nits and flicking them on to the platform. I hot-footed it back behind the counter.

The Director bustled in with her children – a little stressed, pre-holiday exhaustion – not from her months of work beforehand as a producer – but from the military manoeuvres required to pack up a family and get everyone present and correct at the holiday starting point – the coffee shop. We've talked several times. She is a very dynamic lady – a go-getter who is never afraid to say what she is thinking. Qualities I feel compelled to respect, as I watch her grab enough travel snacks to feed an army rather than the children with her – typical travel behaviour. They were heading for the airport, off on what she described as 'a common holiday'. I asked her what she meant. In previous years, the family had gone to relatively exotic destinations guaranteed to attract those all important social media likes, which in turn seem to determine status.

This year her children had asked to have a 'proper' holiday. No disrespect meant on my part, but I didn't understand. Probably none on hers either as she enlightened me. A 'proper holiday' was in fact a 'common' holiday, defined as an all-inclusive hotel with a water slide, and somewhere with a 'Full English' on every restaurant menu. This time her children were happily going with the masses somewhere in Spain.

I smiled politely, but did not wade into the conversation which would have taken hours of debate on issues such as value, appreciation, class, judgement, spoilt children, and EasyJet. There are some St Leonards passengers without the proverbial pot to take to the non-existent toilet – who would love the opportunity to go on holiday anywhere at all, with or without a slide, let alone one in water. There are the Haves and the Have Nots. It's the way of the world, always has been, always will be. And CUT.

As they left on their journey of privilege, I gave some thought to the social structure surrounding St Leonards. It could not be more contradictory. A strong society accepts and thrives on diversity – accepting a certain level of chaos – respecting differences of capacity, ability, thought and interest. I was beginning to understand that St Leonards is a very strong society.

Common as muck, happy as a pig, common as muck, happy as a pig.

Hunger Pang

POLITELY SHY AND on her way to school – her giant, fur-trimmed hood dwarfed her delicate face. School children are not overly welcome in the coffee shop if they come en masse for obvious reasons. Their budgets are limited and motives can be questionable. Like Noah, I am happy to accept well-mannered pairs. Mouthy children with hand gestures and attitude, who snigger while blocking the doorway in their school uniform, are easily traced to a source. I have, on several occasions, phoned one of the local schools with a genuine complaint and an accurate description. This in turn has resulted in the trundling of a gobby little shit back to my counter by their own Headmaster for a solemn and insincere apology. I find this privately amusing – having made so many similar apologies myself in my time – while respecting the schools for taking responsibility for their uniformed pupils in the wider community.

Fur-trim was scanning the counter from a distance.

"Can I help?"
"No, just looking what I can get for 20 pence for school lunch."
"Nothing really – um … did you have breakfast?"
"Not really."
"Well can you get lunch at school?"
"Not really."
I softened.
"There's just you and me here – talk to me?"
"We've got no food at home, Mum couldn't put money on my card. She hasn't got any."

My pang was not hunger related. This job can break your heart sometimes. I have been through financially tough times but have always managed to feed my family. My children laughingly remind me of the day I sent them to school with bread for their lunch. They thought I had forgotten the filling. At least the bread was homemade.

"Here, have this steak pasty, and these snacks – and I will make you a large hot chocolate – no –really – it's fine – keep your 20 pence."

Children in need are not a minority group in St Leonards – under privilege is everywhere. This is why I found the little out-stretched hand offering me the coins so touching – such proud determination to do the right thing – even when in desperate need – and pay as much of her way as she could.

"The train now approaching Platform 1 – Is Delayed." Collective sighing echoed around the station, drowning out the surround-sound tannoy's unwelcome announcement.

Points Mean Prizes

DELAYS AFFECT EVERYONE – I have to admit they can be good for business. However, it is far nicer serving customers who planned to buy something, rather than those who feel forced to because they have no idea how long they will be stranded.

Network Rail is the Godfather of the Railway franchisee and there can be hefty sanctions for delays and cancellations depending on the franchise. My vague and possibly inaccurate understanding is as follows. If a train is cancelled it incurs a big fine. If it arrives at its final destination late, fines are charged per minute late. This probably explains why some trains, when delayed, run fast – miss out stops leaving passengers stranded – in an attempt to reach their final destination as close to the scheduled time as possible – thereby avoiding a pay-out. Not exactly customer friendly.

However, if the delay is caused by the infra-structure– such as point failure or a signalling problem – then the effected Operator can claim a monetary award back from the Godfather. None of which helps the stranded passengers waiting for a fast train to no-where.

"The train now approaching Platform 1 is the 07.47 Southeastern service (blue train) to London Charing Cross calling at West St Leonards, Crowhurst, Battle, Robertsbridge, Etchingham, Stonegate, Wadhurst, Frant, Tunbridge Wells, High Brooms, Tonbridge, Hildenborough, and Sevenoaks…"

The Knole Park oak trees have been replaced several times. In 1902, to commemorate the coronation of King Edward VII – seven oaks were planted on the north side of The Vine cricket ground only to become one oak following the Great Storm of 1987.

Chapter 6

Station Man

MEN AND MY relationships with them have always been problematic. I have no problem attracting them – for whatever reason – whether I want to keep them or whether they want to keep me is a different matter.

I have a track record for a bad boy – and whereas I have had more than my fair share of opportunity to sit with my hair in foils – I have always run for the hills. Henley-on-Thames was my playground for my twenties – a designer town with its own Riviera. It is also the home of the pompous prat. The Chairman was an exception. He had fallen for my sultry, silent self. I had been out one Friday to a roof-top bar near Marlow – driven there by a prat to meet up with a group of 'friends', which included The Chairman.

I was inappropriately dressed – another track record of mine – and sat there listening to polite, correct conversation – my eyes were flashing – my inner boredom suggested an uprising – feigning migraine – *"oh sweetie"* – *"you poor thing"* – clutching my head to avoid banging it on the table as I slowly lost the will. Prat offered to drive me back but I protested about not wishing to ruin his evening and persuaded him to let me take taxi. A successful and welcome escape. Hot footing it home – I phoned a partner in crime – shimmied into nightime clothing and we bowled through the doors of Stallone's – Henley's version of Stringfellows – straight into the group I had left at the bar. Awkward – but only if you give a shit.

The Chairman gave a shit – he pushed me up against a wall to kiss me as we fell out through a fire-exit causing the alarms to go off. My second escape of the evening – involving scrabbling over a security wall into the night. The Chairman was exciting and unpredictable. He took me to Holland later in the week. Having business to attend to he dropped me somewhere in Amsterdam – handed me five grand to shop with and told me to meet him at 3pm. I spent a fiver on two cups of coffee – always essential – and threw the remaining money back at him when he returned. Wanker. His amusement turned to respect. We had a good time. His passion was boats but he also loved a fast car. We flung a Porsche round the Nurburgring – both getting off on the rush. He posted a plane ticket to New York through my door – one of the best weekends of my life. He was already there and met me in a limousine from JFK. We got pissed in the afternoon at Pier 6 – did the Empire, Waldorf, Bloomingdales, Chinatown, Statue of Liberty – I had a panic attack in her crown causing me to hold up a coachload of Japanese tourists who were stuck in her neck and far too polite to shove me up the arse and out of the way. The weekend ended with a show on Broadway. The only souvenir I brought back was a cheap, plastic, statue replica – he presented it to me on the plane home. I still have it in my box marked treasure.

I didn't know it that Friday night in Marlow – but also in that group was an absolute diamond – she is to this day one of my handful of long standing female friends – so I really should be grateful to the prat who introduced me to both of them. Henley boys are fun to play with – but I would advise against marrying one – unless of course your aspiration is a head full of foils.

'Could I have a cappuccino please?'
'Of course – it's a miserable day.'
'Isn't it.'
I wondered why she had sandals on.

Station Man – tall, dark and handsome and I wanted to shag him – I probably would. I knew him from a different track – out looking for business development not romantic involvement. Having already identified the potential of a coffee shop with a captive market, Station Man held the key to let me in.

We had a mutual attraction the first time we met – just something about him. He was standing too close to me as we compared a bag of new edition pound coins. Chatting easily, I suddenly had an overwhelming desire to kiss him. Something was sparking. Kissing – a very level and intimate playing field – one I always choose to detach from while keeping my eyes wide open. I didn't appreciate this unwelcome invasion of feeling and switched abruptly back into business mode.

Driving home I realised it had been a while since I allowed myself to feel this way – not the shagging part – the kissing. Kissing is too personal – maybe the mouth is the route to the mind – and anything covering it is some kind of censorship. So why did I kiss him? Deciding to treat the stomach fluttering as indigestion – I cranked up the music to loud and floored it. Can't be many women in their fifties who still blow their car speakers. Driving fast to loud music calms me – it focuses my mind and helps me think. I know this is reckless. I can be.

Persistence pays. Flirtatious texts make chemistry. Dates make history. The age gap was cougar fashionable – I thought he was older – he thought I was younger – we cracked on regardless. We had a blast – easy in our own company – compatible in our thinking. It had all the ingredients of a successful relationship. Inevitably life – both past and present – will get in the way. His past was giving him a good kicking whereas mine was long since squared away – at least on the surface. Too many complications too early on – before the foundations have had a chance to set – typically result in an implosion. As I get older I find I have even less tolerance for problems outside a relationship that break in and consume it.

Independence can be a burden – but it's the state I always choose. I find myself highly dependable and life is safer on your own – less complicated – more efficient. Sex is important to me – but commitment – like I said – I can't do it. I am already over-extended – emotionally, mentally, financially and physically. Privately I was falling for him. I knew he had fallen for me. But beware the defensive lover when she becomes offensive.

Don't barrage me with kindness, softness, feelings of love and affection – because I will take these as weakness and be inclined to walk all over you – as I start to lose respect and you start to hate me. I prefer to hang out with bad-boys anyway – enjoying the ride –comfortable in the certainty that it will end at any moment. I know where I am that way. No expectations – no disappointment. I'm good at many things – relationships are not one of them. Was I the reason? Who cares – just keep turning the music up until the thoughts are drowned out.

Station Man went away to resolve his own complications – he told me it would be alright in the end. I knew it wouldn't be. We walked away from each other – both of us hurting. Slaps sting and the residual pain is dull. A reminder of why I don't do love or commitment. Station Man – probably a mistake. But I thank him for the memories, one very special Easter Sunday, and a revised definition of passion. I have no time for regrets as I am too busy being a realist rather than a romantic.

For the dream for the lesson, for the dream for the lesson, how many more bloody lessons?

A Minute on the Lips – A Life-time on the Hips

'I fancy something to eat but I'm trying to be good – too fat.'
'You look fine to me.'
'I am but my partner's always going on at me about weight.'
'Get a new one.'

Customer snacking habits are fascinating. Days of the week are the barometer of habit indicators. Please bear in mind that I am not laughing at my customers but laughing with them – because like so many, I too start the week resolute.

On Mondays it's all about health, Warrior 2, avocado and being mindful or mindless and drinking enough water to drown your own body weight. 'My Body Is A Temple' Monday is followed by semi-skimmed Tuesday. Thereafter follows oatmeal and raisin cookie Wednesday, a little dip in the water of fresh pastry Thursday, and then suddenly it is Full Fat Friday. Sausage rolls, pastries, caramel shortcakes, sugary cokes – never mind the tax, syrup shots in everything and potato crisps not banana ones. Gluten free last seen getting on the slow train to nowhere for a dirty weekend with vegan. We all love the weekends – where anything goes – because weekday rules are thrown straight out of the window and impulse takes hold.

The weather – well it goes without saying but in hot weather customers tend to eat less and drink lots of water – chocolate stays in the fridge – but more crisps are consumed – probably in an attempt to replace the salt lost from the energy expended walking up to or down from the station – or cure the hangover brought on by the over-indulgence the night before. St Leonards is a party town after all – Pirates Day, Fat Tuesday, Jack on The Green, Frost Fairs, any excuse to overdo it.

Customers buy snacks to celebrate. Chocolate because they are happy, sad, or bored waiting for a train. Chocolate – because they deserve it – because work is so stressful. Chocolate as a consolation for the lost argument, the promotion, the broken heart. Chocolate – just the ticket.

Making healthy choices has never been so difficult – so much information – so much choice. Gluten free, paleo, no dairy, soya, almond, protein – lots of protein – sugar disguising itself as a cereal bar, nuts, more protein. I stock it all.

Then … there is the second barometer known as guilt. This is where men and women are so different. Men take a view – if they want it they will have it – end of. No debate, no discussion, no hesitation, no 'I shouldn't really' tedious interrogations about whether it is the right lifestyle choice for them to make at that particular moment in time, no 'will I regret it for the rest of my day/week/month/year or life'. Men just have it.

Women – oh my goodness – we are our own worst enemy. Take a pew – delay the train – it's going to be a long decision – cookie or chocolate? Brownie or crisps? Or nothing. Most of us feel we shouldn't on a regular basis – whether we do is a personal choice

– usually deeply personal – based on appearance and weight loss – it is seldom about weight gain. The discussions and deliberations I have heard, the really rather pathetic justifications I have listened to as the resolve weakens – carbs and sugar victorious – as the woman accepts defeat while vowing to do better next time. There is always a next time.

We have become conditioned over the years to believe that thin is beautiful. It is probably now more politically correct to say that thin is healthy and healthy is good. We all know beauty comes from within – from within a size 10 anyway. There have been many a campaign championing the plus, encouraging you to love the skin you are in.

The belief that thin is beautiful is now a fundamental part of society – teenage indoctrination fuelled on by social media filters. We can blame Instagram, miniscule designer labels, advertising, perception or my grandmother – but we only have ourselves to blame for the brainwashing. There is healthy and then there is unrealistic. I was borderline anorexic in my early twenties – eating minimal calories 3 days a week – exercising furiously for the rest of it. Throughout my life I have had a love-hate relationship with food and exercise. It began with the untimely death of my father and the acceptance into the affluent social scene of Henley-On-Thames – where money means power which in turn surrounds itself with beautiful things – some of which are objects and some of which are slender young women. Sorry, feminists of the world unite – but tell me that is not how it is? Nowadays it can only be described as ambitious to leave me alone in a room with a Battenberg cake and ask me not to eat it.

After years of self-obsessing, I have inadvertently (fucked up) passed on my food issues to my children and I am furious with myself for doing so. My weight, rather than my achievements, was always a central topic at family reunions. I lived much of my adult life addicted to the gym – before walking away – physically exhausted. My children are now super fit. I probably should get back on the lycra waggon – and I will do – when I am ready – but quite frankly at the moment I can't be arsed. Hamish, my youngest, gives me a bollocking if he finds evidence of cake or wine in the house. Feeling the need for a glass of full-bodied red one Friday night without the third degree from the alcohol police – I poured a glass and went and sat on the downstairs toilet with the door shut. Heaven … until the door flung open. *"Have you any idea how sad you look?"* was the disgusted comment. Oh, the shame, the guilt – and the advantage of not having a mirror in the downstairs loo. His policing used to irritate me – but now I understand. He does this because he loves me – and because he is terrified of me dying early – because I am all he has.

I did not eat then. I do eat now. Because thin was beautiful, thin was in control. I loved being a size 10 – but nobody loved being around me while I maintained the discipline required to sustain it. Now I am in control – and accept I am larger – having learnt that allowing diet and exercise to become an obsession is actually detrimental to your health. Is it normal to exercise 21 hours a week and congratulate yourself for ending every day with a calorie deficit? My body took the punishment my mind delivered. Sentence served. Today I freely admit that sometimes I like cake – and in the case of a Battenberg – the whole cake and nothing but the cake. Ipso fatso. Everything in moderation – rather than deprivation. So, I stand with the men. Have it.

"Stand well away from the edge of the platform. The approaching train is not scheduled to stop at this station and will pass at speed."

Paid Staff

THE COFFEE SHOP was holding its own – I had exhausted all favours along with myself – it was time to recruit a more permanent member of staff. Harder than you might think. Staff are the biggest asset and the biggest headache for any employer. I had learnt many hard lessons of employment along the way and worked for some miserable bastards. What is wrong with work being fun? I have a sense of humour and a really good laugh is such a great tonic. I am pretty laid back, provided the actual work is done and the customers remain the priority. After all, the very nature of the coffee shop counter means it is approachable – conversation is actively encouraged. Nobody wants to be served anything by someone with a face like a slapped arse – and it's equally dull when a customer presents with one (there is always the imaginary slap to fantasize about if we need to).

There is a fine art to managing staff effectively – happy, loved staff are loyal and dependable – too much love and you run the risk of them taking the piss. Fine lines are fine because staff are people, with problems, emotions and feelings. I am flattered that they feel comfortable enough to let me in to their own lives and I help them where I can – or straight-talk when I can't. Talking fixes most things. Something I understand in my professional live but don't apply to my private one.

I care about the staff. I understand the importance of investing in people and the importance of feeling valued. At the coffee shop, we have become inter-dependant – forming our own small counter community.

Roberto (Spanish please, not Italian) was my first permanent member of staff – introduced to me by mutual friends. He had barista experience and needed to subsidise his artist's income. He became a favourite with the early morning commuters, who learnt to accept his unorthodox approach to life – as did I. He served them perfect coffee ('rrregoolar' or 'large') with a dazzling smile. His sharp wit was softened by his thick accent. Highly intelligent in at least four languages, always immaculate and always on time. (Time anxiety?) He was an Artist who eventually left me, following an inexplicable tantrum, to study at the Royal College of London.

On occasion, behind the counter, a lightening flash of the Latino temperament broke through. Some customers complained he was arrogant and rude. Sometimes he probably was – but like me – he does not suffer fools, gladly or otherwise. Luckily for all – the coffee shop location means a tricky customer only has a finite time to punish us before their train comes in – and we are off the hook until next time – unless that customer happens to be Harriet Harpie. Roberto and Harpie had numerous countertop clashes.

"Who is that dreadful woman?"
"You mean Harriet Harpie?"
"I made her four coffees and she complained about every single one. I told her to make her mind up before she comes in next time – is that ok? She was making me ab-so-lute-ly crazy."

Roberto's pet hate was bad manners which upset him in various ways:
Please do not take hold of the cookie jar tongs and attempt to help yourself. Staff only.
Please do not unscrew the cap of a drink and consume it before you pay for it. You might steal it.
Please do not buy food and stand in front of him eating it with your mouth open.
Please do not ever do that it is simply disgusting.
Please do not come in here high on drugs on a Sunday morning – or any other morning for that matter – and expect him to deal with

you. Because then he phones me and I have to deal with all of you.

His favourite customer was the Viking. He loved the Viking. I loved the Viking. A drop dead gorgeous, refined and rugged, ripped and torn, bronzed and chiselled Australian brick-layer. We both drooled over the Viking. Nothing was too much trouble for him. Cold milk, lids off, anything at all. I am confident that The Viking would have been permitted to use the cookie tongs, open a cold drink before paying for it, and stand in front of the counter eating with his mouth open and definitely with his shirt off – or lounging with his feet up on the pew if he wanted to. But he was far too well-mannered because he was perfect.

Roberto used to text me when The Viking had been in – he was his early morning fix – the coffee shop guilty pleasure. The over-excitement of his appearance was counter-balanced with a green tea detox and some yoga. The Viking just made the mornings so much better. I wonder if he ever knew the impact he had. Such a shame that he returned down under.

Roberto and I had a strange relationship. Boss/employee, sister/ brother, shepherd/sheep. He had a vulnerability few people saw. Emotionally damaged but charming and insightful. He became very defensive when challenged about anything and quick to attack. I find myself drawn to damaged people – some kind of internal radar – I like to fix them. It makes them feel better and allows me to feel good about myself.

Modern Art

WE DID HAVE one particularly heated situation across the counter involving unsolicited criticism of his art. I displayed it as a favour and got mixed reactions from the customers. Art is, after all, subjective.

I know all about the texture and layering of his paintings and how long it takes to produce the desired effect, because Roberto educated me at length (or to death) on the subject. I also understand that to one person's eye, deep Mediterranean blue paintings of subtly different shades and depth of layering evoke certain things to one person and completely different things to another – as we were all about to discover.

Roberto often stayed on after a shift chatting to me in half lotus position about the meaning of life. This particular day, young Kelly walked in with her mother. She is the star of a well-known TV programme, but respecting her right to anonymity I never alluded to it – despite her wearing the name of the TV series on her jacket. Kelly decided to critique the paintings. *"That is not art,"* she said. *"I could draw that, anybody could paint like that. It's just blue paint dragged all over the canvas."*

Deadly silence – then the Latino fire started to rise. Beneath the high counter I slowly made a flagging gesture with my left hand – urging Roberto to calm down – hoping the other side of the counter could not see it and that their train would arrive on time. It did – and the second they were out of the door Roberto exploded. Apoplectic with fury, he unleashed his wrath about the ignorance of children and the fact that she had no idea – and then he changed tack – enthusiastically blaming her mother – *"After all"*, he said, *"as my grandmother would say"*, (I know his grandmother used to say a lot – it was a favourite saying of his), *"it is hard to know which of the two are the most uneducated – the daughter for obviously making loud statements about things she is too young to understand, let alone appreciate – or the mother for being so ignorant as to not stop her daughter from making the statements in the first place – showing them both to be uneducated and stupid."*

Sometimes I have to use diplomatic skills worthy of a United Nations summit. I have learnt to say nothing. Soothing noises are frequently deemed to be patronising and can re-kindle a fire.

Roberto may have been a touch temperamental but he left behind his legacy – a lesson in dedication. He got up at 4.30 am every day to walk in to work – 45 minutes door to door – whatever the month, whatever the weather. He was late once – I only remember because it was once – and he was devastated about it for days – his anxiety had a greater meaning than time. I find the cold quite bracing in a jolly hockey sticks, character building kind of way. Warm-blooded Roberto hated it. The coffee shop has a permanently open front door policy in more ways than one. To cope with the cold, he made a fashion statement of wearing his entire jumper collection at the same time – and looked good wearing multiple beanies. No matter what the weather, he was always dependable. I miss him – and the pornographic texts he used to send me by mistake – meant for his lover the morning after the night before!

Canine Commuters

NOT ALL COMMUTERS are human. I was surprised to discover how many dogs do their fair share of the daily commute. There would have to be an emergency on a global scale for me to consider taking my Labradors on a train. They are well behaved in their own environment but could be guaranteed to do a huge dump in the middle of the carriage – or something equally horrific – because dogs – like children have a tendency to show you up when you need it the least.

My other observation is that canine commuters can be as temperamental as human ones. Although maybe they are just mirroring their owners. Some sulk when the weather is foul. Some foul when the weather is fine. Some simply object to being at the station and grumble to those who can hear them at platform level. Some never put a paw wrong – trained to commute to perfection.

I always know when the French bull dog is commuting – I can hear him huffing and puffing – waiting for his owner who orders a regular 'what is the point' coffee – a half shot decaff soya cappuccino with no chocolate – to everyone your side of the counter. I have learnt that French bull dogs are prone to breathing difficulties and cannot be over exerted – rather like a teenager when asked to tidy a bedroom.

I would just like to take this opportunity to name and shame the owner of the Liver Spaniel. Do not come into the coffee shop again with your dog, then just stand there watching while it cocks its leg all over my platform sign – yes, the one right outside the shop entrance, the one that is carried inside by my hands at the end of the day. I mean … really??

Lastly, whilst on the subject of animal travellers, a friendly warning to passengers unfamiliar with the familiar goings on at St Leonards. On occasion, you may see a ferret on a lead on Platform 1. Ferrets can be irritable. If boarding the same carriage – I advise allowing the owner to sit in the ferret's favourite seat, which is probably everyone's, the forward-facing window seat. I have been advised that the ferret prefers his view of the fields without the sun in his eyes as he reminisces of quarries gone by.

"The train now approaching platform 1 is the 10.45 Southern service (green train) to Brighton calling at Bexhill, Collington, Cooden Beach, Normans Bay, Pevensey Bay, Pevensey and Westham …"

Pevensey Bay is the settlement where William the Conqueror made the landing for his invasion of England in 1066. The Normans introduced chivalry to English leaders who were prone to murdering their rivals. Apparently, on his death his bowels burst as monks tried to force his fat form into a stone sarcophagus – rather like putting on jeans from a tumble dryer.

Chapter 7

Miami Vice

SOME CUSTOMERS PUT me on edge. I sense their unpredictability and wonder which way it will go. Most of the time I am able to keep the conversation neutral with a gentle steer, silently praying for their train to roll in. There is no point antagonising the antagonistic – even though I want to tell them to fuck off – it would inevitably prolong their presence. Years ago, I wouldn't have stopped to think twice – happy to argue the toss till the cow went home. Today I am mature and moderately respectable.

St Leonards has a resident dominatrix – she is mildly terrifying – distinctive by her spurs and furry hats. I hope she doesn't sit next to the ferret on the train. There is a place and a use for spurs. She probably knows of a couple I don't. She is a hard-nosed loose cannon – always angling for opportunity. Her favourite saying is 'the more powerful the man, the more painful the punishment'. She had a particular client who paid to be cast in Plaster of Paris and chained up in her dungeon for the weekend. This raised another unwelcome and practical conversation about toilets – but I was assured that she left two gaps in strategic places and was generous enough to move a bucket around. Paraphilia is the umbrella term for defining sexual deviance – fetishism, exhibitionism, voyeurism, masochism etc. – no doubt Mistress Miami will have a solution for these 'isms' – which may or may not involve the umbrella.

She caters for all – I reluctantly concede we possibly have that in common. I wonder why she is so proud to dominate – to effectively abuse clients – albeit consensual – and at what point in her life did her switch flick? I think the bigger point here is that her clients are paying her to get off while doing so themselves – it's a route of enquiry I decided not to pursue – I know she would have been happy to explain in graphic detail – I have imagination.

She told me that she began her dominatrix career overseas. By day she worked in an office – she started whipping out of boredom – made a small fortune. I always sigh with relief when she leaves and the coffee shop remains unscathed.

Sex – a counter conversation somewhere all the time. Because as a society, we are fascinated with it. Although why we should be fascinated with the sex lives of others could in itself be seen as bordering on deviance – or is it fascination for comparison purposes? – desperate for a benchmark – or reassurance that one's personal sex life is as good as all media dictates it should be? I believe it was Freud who said 'sexual investigation and intellectual investigation go hand in hand.' I do not feel the need to challenge him on that particular observation.

Sex can also be the reason for a train ride. An elderly customer had a meltdown in my shop because his train was delayed. He kept rushing in and out muttering like a March Hare, *"Oh dear, oh dear, oh dear, I'm late, I'm late, I'm late..."*, until he burst into tears. I wasn't expecting that. I offered my assistance and discreetly passed a couple of napkins his way. *"I need to get to London Victoria – I am meeting someone and have been looking forward to it for ages."* I helped him re-route to a different station and he asked if I would kindly phone his friend to arrange his collection – which I did – kindly. *"Thank you so much, you have no idea what this means –we've arranged to have a 3-way."* My jaw dropped.

Sex has always been a personal choice – and even though as a society we will always remain obsessed with the sex lives of others – we should really only be interested in our own – as it is the only one that has any real relevance. Sex is like cake – I like cake – and in the case of some cakes – the whole cake and nothing but the cake – ipso fuckso – not necessarily in moderation – never through deprivation. So, again, I stand with the men. Have it!

Crack of the whip, crack of the whip, crack of the whip, crack of the whip.

Cow Juice

'Do you have any other kind of milk?'

Hail the new trend – the mushrooming of veganism. Soya has fallen out of fashion already – only to be replaced with oat, almond, and coconut. At least the liquid inside a coconut is officially known as milk. Oat is a cereal. How do you know you are about to serve a vegan? Because they tell you at length, possibly hoping to recruit you to join the movement, impervious to the queue forming behind them. Commercial instinct has forced me to accept the trend and eat into my margins as I stock these milk alternatives.

Milk is something most of us take for granted. Produced by mammals to feed their young – production stops at weaning. Humans persist in drinking the milk of other species – with little thought of where it comes from. If we stopped to think about it in more depth – we might be put off its consumption. I am not. I personally do not like cereal or beans floating about in my coffee – call me a traditionalist – but alternative milks seem to activate my gag reflex. My daughter has joined the trend – you have no idea how much it pains me to put the carton in the trolley.

As with any product – a surge in popularity always means a price hike by suppliers – I used not to charge – but the costs are such that I now have to pass them on to my customers. Here is a little test for R&D purposes. As I now charge you extra to join the trend – do you enjoy paying more because it makes you feel superior or do you feel ripped off? If you are happy to pay then I will concede that you actually prefer it. If you have a genuine allergy, I am of course sympathetic. If you are deliberately being pretentious, then just have the milk. You are embarrassing yourself.

'Sorry – no toilets at St Leonards.'
'What living hell must we endure?'

Public Convenience

THERE ARE NO public toilets at St Leonards Warrior Square Station. I repeat – there are no toilets at St Leonards Station – no public toilets – not one. Today I kept a little tally by the till – the total toilet enquiries for today topping out at 84. That is 84 desperate travellers looking for a public convenience. Some accept the pleasant 'sorry' – others want a public enquiry about the inconvenience.

'What do you do then?'
'Not that my business is your business – I use the staff toilet in the booking office.'

'Can I use it?' – 'Are you staff?'
'How can I use the disabled toilet?'
'You need a radar key from the Council as a registered disabled person.'
'But I'm not disabled.'
'It's a miracle! – but you still can't use the toilet.'
'Blimey – no toilets *anywhere* on the station? FFS.'
'Well I won't have a coffee if I can't use a toilet.'

Well don't then, that is your choice to make not mine – but I do understand if it is in fact a deal breaker.

'No toilets? Are you having a laugh?' (If only.)
'No, sorry, there are no toilets on the station but there will be one on the train (it may or may not be operational – but it will at least exist).'

It does not matter how many times you ask me, protest, swear, comment analyse, sigh, eye roll, fake shock horror, nod in quiet acceptance, then immediately ask me again out of sheer desperation, explain about your bladder problems, your partner's hospital appointments, tell me how much liquid you have drunk today – it does not change the situation. When you shout at me, it makes me hope you wet yourself. Childish I know – but true.

Neighbouring establishments have toilets for paying customers only. Herein lies a small moral dilemma for me. If I direct you somewhere with a toilet, I potentially lose a sale. I see the anguish in your eyes, as you move discreetly from one foot to the other. Elderly people are genuinely fearful of having a public accident – always quick to share intimate bladder history with me in the hope that I can magic up a cubicle. Sometimes it's the frantic hopping of a child with the mother – knowing time is of the essence – or in one case – just too late.

As I am a kind-hearted soul and to minimise the risk of accidents on the shop floor – my dilemma is relatively short lived as I point them in the direction of the King's Road. What has surprised me is the number of them who have returned to purchase a coffee out of gratitude. There will always be those who were never looking for anything other than a toilet – not even a train.

In the booking hall – like a mirage in the facility-free desert where we work – is one firmly locked disabled toilet, which sits there gloating behind the door – a porcelain throne – denied to all the miserable, cross-legged, able-bodied passengers. The sign states 'Only Holders of the Radar Key May Pass' – a bladder buster rather than a Hollywood blockbuster. Perhaps there will be a sequel … or perhaps we will leave it there.

On a serious note, disabled people know how to obtain a radar key. Desperately needing to go to the toilet may feel somewhat disabling but it does not actually qualify – and unless you have a key – you are not going in there.

The toilets were removed long before my time – a drug user's paradise. The public toilets outside the station were 'condemned' more recently. Rumours are rife but there are currently no plans for reinstatement – perhaps the passengers could start an RMT (Return My Throne) campaign. All I know is that absolutely everyone who asks about them – or overhears the conversation from the pew or the doorway – all agree the toilets should make a come-back. The rumours at least give the community a sense of hope.

Transition Town Hastings Project

'Four teas please with milk and a large white coffee and one cappuccino – and could we borrow a tray to get it over the footbridge? – we are working on the garden.'
'Yes of course …' and silently I know I am kissing goodbye to the tray.

Communities need hope and something to feel good about. This project delivers both. A very hard-working group of volunteers swapped rubble and overgrown brambles for idealism, raised beds and vegetables, for the benefit of all, no money required. They created a community garden on Platform 2 – directly opposite the coffee shop. As the garden becomes more established, the fruit bushes and flowers will flourish. A simple concept – a garden created by the community for the community. All produce is free to all – just help yourself on your way past. Anyone is welcome to volunteer. My excellent vantage point allows me to observe the garden surviving the test of time, developing peacefully, free of vandalism. Another great indicator of the true sense of community spirit at St Leonards.

Then a hideous 'proposal' bench arrived – probably to give the hard-working volunteers somewhere to sit and admire the fruit of their labour. My initial understanding was that it served as a marriage proposal bench. This struck me as a risqué location choice – in the event of unforeseen rejection, the train tracks could be deemed frighteningly close. I am always apprehensive when I see a couple sitting on it – but I misunderstood – the bench is there for people to sit on while writing a proposal – about what I am not entirely sure.

I have watched enough DIY Changing Room type programmes to know that the back of an old wardrobe nailed between two tall pieces of 2 x 4 – will always look like the back of an old wardrobe. I like the idea – not the end result – which I can see all day long as it is right opposite my open door. Another rustic bench has made an appearance next to the raised beds – far more in keeping with the tone of the Project. Agree to disagree while praying for a brutally windy day to blow one away.

On a serious note – we could all learn a lot from this Project. Society is an abstract concept – it exists in the minds of individuals who form part of it. People create places. A concrete community is built by people finding common ground within their geographical proximity. It gives its members a sense of belonging. This Project voluntarily gives up free time and energy to create something for the common good of the community. Some of the best interactions in life are had at grass-roots level. If you strip back the rough outer layers of St Leonards and look more closely – you will find an extraordinary depth of community here – people from all walks of life – interrelated – co-dependant – with nothing and everything in common. My coffee shop exists because of the support of this community – a fact I gratefully respect.

One final request – could the piñatas be removed from the trees? Over time they look like toilet paper that has been blown into branches – and the one thing we most certainly do not need at this particular station are any more references to toilets.

"Vehicles parked at unauthorized points may be clamped or removed without warning. Short and long stay parking is available at this station."

Repent at Leisure

'Cup of arsenic please.'
'Do you mean americano?'
'Debatable.'

'Are you alright?
'I'm fine.'
'You don't look fine – sit on the pew – I will bring your tea.'

I remember the first time this polite but sad lady came into the coffee shop with her well behaved children in tow. She was in her forties – prime time for divorce – in the same way that men in their fifties are in prime time for redundancy. She brought with her the welcome suggestion of a lending library for the window sill and a couple of bags of books to start it off.

She wasn't feeling well but was determined to struggle in to her London-based job. Why? Guilt or fear that one too many sick days will jeopardise her job? I do not allow sick staff to work – obviously there are Environmental Health rules that have to be adhered to – but I selfishly don't want to catch their germs myself.

A tearful conversation concluded that her husband had run off with a younger model – yawn. Men can be so predictable. Like apes, they cannot let go of one branch until they have hold of another. Women aren't afraid of falling – we take in the view on the way down. Beauty is a shallow beast. Those younger models will eventually get bored – when his backside becomes triangular and his wallet much lighter – because divorce can be a nasty bitch.

Once love has gone for one – it has effectively gone for both. Long drawn out arguments only line the pockets of the divorce lawyer vulture. Few couples seem able to divorce amicably – opting instead for bitter arguments over marriage memorabilia. Starting relationships are easy – the process of ending them – labyrinths of destruction – proceed quickly with caution. No party lasts for ever.

I was married once – and what a mistake that was. I have always had a thing about the Wild West. I booked in to a dude ranch for my 30th birthday, somewhere in the Colorado Rockies, in an attempt to get it out of my system. Instead, I fell in love with the mountains and the simplicity of ranch life. I have no problem being dominated by nature.

I spent my actual birthday evening camping out in a mountain meadow after riding all day through the Rockies. My life was at a crossroads – nothing new there – and I decided to unburden to a stranger – a wrangler called Josh. He could only take so much – and in the small hours he declared his surrender – *"Ma'am – could you quit your bitchin'?"* he drawled – and I roared with laughter. Wranglers do not provide counselling services.

Life had been challenging – putting myself through university as a mature student. I had a mortgage and a job prior to studying and was used to having an income. To support myself, I set up as a freelance proof-reader/editor armed with a copy of the Writers and Artists Year Book and a computer. The internet was only just making its debut – I wrote to all the publishers – and to my surprise – got a fair amount of work – hand written manuscripts and edits were still very much in existence.

I was invited to attend a meeting at the head office of a famous children's book publisher. They needed an editor/proof reader for a small series of books. I borrowed a briefcase – chucked in my Walkman and a packet of Marlboro and pitched up as requested. Horrified, I was shown to a huge meeting room with an oval table – the entire team were at the meeting. I appeared sufficiently knowledgeable, the job was mine and I was given a huge pile of manuscripts to take away with me. Too embarrassed to open the case and reveal the pathetic contents inside – I fiddled with the lock – pretending it was broken – refused offers of help from an office screwdriver and made my escape.

When I wasn't editing or studying – I was barmaiding – I loved working at the pub – escapism from books and screens – the banter was good and the tips were better.

My passion for the Wild West led me to apply for a job on a prestigious ranch high up in the Zirkel Wilderness, Steamboat Springs, Colorado. I finished my degree and jumped on a plane in search of the Marlboro Man – having turned down a seriously starchy, corporate opportunity in Edinburgh. Ranching was a dream job for me. Hanging out in the great outdoors – taking rides out across the Rockies – driving cattle back down to the Homestead – fixing fences and chopping wood – before serving guests in the dining room in the evening – where the guys got hard listening to my accent. That is where I met my husband – and that is where I should have left him. But I didn't – even when my close girlfriends told me to.

Instead – I married him – in England – nobody was more shocked than I was. Because of all the suitors past and present – I probably loved him the least. Maybe I was clinging on to my ranch-hand days – it's easy to overlook imperfections when you reinvent yourself overseas. We took over a pub in leafy Berkshire straight after our wedding.

I had several counter conversations in the coffee shop with Large Marge – she used to run a London boozer during the IRA bombings – she had seen some harsh things in her life. She was having a tough time – dividing herself between her elderly mother stuck in a Brighton nursing home and her husband in a local dementia home – terrified every time her mobile rang that someone had died. She told me she was planning to go on a cruise when they both died and, when on board, she would fling her phone over the side.

"Well quite frankly", she said, *"my husband was bloody useless."* Mine was always drunk. *"At the first sign of trouble in the boozer – he used to trundle me out to sort all the bother."* As did mine.

My landlady days did not go well – the village was hostile and he was drinking heavily. We had inadvertently (fucked up so badly) taken over a late-night drinking hole – the bar was rammed on opening night – and when I rang time – all smug with legal knowledge from my law degree – the bar went silent and I thought I was going to be lynched. The village waged a war – bricked the windows frequently and carted the pub sign away in the middle of the night. I hated having my name above the door – running a pub and popping in for a few part-time shifts and a flirt are two very different things.

I did not know much about alcoholism or drunk rage blackouts. I had never needed to. I got into bed one night and heard my husband kicking off in the bar downstairs. Listening to my sixth sense – I crept out of bed and made it to my car – as I started to drive he realised I was leaving and started punching the car roof – I floored it and took refuge at my sister's till dawn. I braved a return to the pub – what a mess – he had smashed up everything – plates – furniture – bottles – everything. I crunched over the glass into the kitchen and there laid out with perfect precision were his chef knives. My blood ran cold – did I just have a lucky escape?

Because I need to fix people – and presuming he had done a runner – I searched until I found him in departures at Heathrow airport. He had been knocked over by a car – I hope it hurt. Forlorn and broken – he admitted he was an alcoholic and returned to the States to begin his recovery.

Back at the pub, I sat alone in the bar, pregnant with our first child and analysed the situation I was in. I got a distinct sinking feeling. The bricks kept flying in through the windows – the phone calls kept coming from America. I should have walked away – but instead I tried to honour my commitment – after all – fixing other people is what I do best. The village got their pub back – and I returned to Colorado. Life was calm – we had two more children – moved to Japan – and then the turbulence returned – worse than ever before. I engineered a move back to the UK – home territory – a perfect location to end a battle.

I knew it was time to divorce when I watched my husband sleeping. I had a fantasy moment with a pillow in my hand – not of a sexual nature. Instead, loving my freedom and knowing he wasn't worth the crime – I went downstairs. While he slept I found him a fabulous job in Alaska. Time for him go home. The job application was clearly a personal best – as they flew him out there and offered him the job – and an easy way out of the marriage for both of us.

I drove him to Heathrow, bought him a coffee (travel essential) and waved him off. We both knew it was the end. I cried all the way to … Windsor – which is not actually that far from Heathrow.

I married quickly to an emotionally unavailable partner. I suppose he did too. An alcoholic's first love never dies. Maybe I chose to ignore the drinking and enjoy the honeymoon phase before reality kicked in. During my marriage, I grieved for a loss – namely my freedom. I admit my marriage was doomed from the start – I consciously married the wrong person. Subconsciously, this was probably another deliberate act of sabotage on my part – fearing the engulfment that marriage inevitably brings in some form or another.

Divorce was the light at the end of a tunnel of mind games and misery – I ran headlong out into the open – taking my beautiful children with me. Whereas I struggle with relationship commitment – motherhood lioness comes naturally to me – committed to my territory – our blood is thick – I will always be there for them. We are all we have. I do not believe in happy ever afters and avoid proposals like the plague.

"The train now departing from Platform 1 is the Southeastern service (blue train) calling at all the chapters in your life that you may or may not wish to re-visit."

Kasia

I WAS INSTANTLY worried. She stood at the counter, jaw locked in a resolute way – but she didn't fool me. Long, white blonde hair, model figure, beautiful angular face and eyes full of turmoil. Desperate for coffee and water – too much red wine the night before with her partner, was her explanation. I hadn't asked.

Her hands were shaking a little bit. She had some time before her train. I knew she was not ok – sensing her partner was the problem – I asked her directly. I can't help myself – if I hear a cry for help, however faint, my inner warrior has to answer it.

Man trouble – ten years her senior – struggling to share her with their young son – he wanted her all to himself. Possession is dark. She fiercely protected him, adamant that he was at least a good father. Why do women do that – fiercely protect the abuser? She was scared – relationship fear – isolating and terrifying – unless you find your voice and cite the slow burn effect (R v Ahluwalia – a domestic abuse game changer) – mind the gap!

Kasia was foreign and had made England her home – but had not been allowed to make a friendship group and had no extended family to draw strength from. It is hard to leave with nowhere to go. She was allowed to work as a carer. Ironic, because somebody desperately needed to take care of her. Trapped by choice or necessity by the two men in her life. Sensing her fear – I had my own – that underneath her pristine white turtle neck lay a multitude of physical and mental bruises.

Several battered women have passed through – the lucky ones on their way to a new life, a new identity. The conversations I have had with them are painful. I know the difference between someone who is having a drama and someone who has become the drama.

I despise men who abuse women. I despise women who abuse men. Abuse is a power struggle that can be defeated by an uprising. Kasia was someone's daughter – where was her lioness? Where was I when an abusive predator went for my daughter right under my nose? I may have been one step behind for a while – but now I am one step in front – the arsehole loaded his own gun – I am confident he will pull the trigger all by himself – I no longer feel the need to witness its discharge.

I feel the same way about prostitution. Let me be very clear – I am not drawing a parallel between abuse and prostitution – they just happen to be two specific issues brought to the forefront of my mind by meeting Kasia. Prostitutes – St Leonards has its share – one or two come through the station on their way to an arrangement. I am not making a judgment here about sugar babies or the sex worker trade. If this is what a woman genuinely chooses to do for her living, fully informed, fully aware and fully conscious – then I have no issue with that. But when women are desperate, run by men, or other women – forced, coerced and terrorised – I have a huge issue with that. They are all somebody's baby girl, sugar-coated or otherwise, and were hopefully once the apple of somebody's eye – rather than the dirty glint in the eye of predatory scum.

Abuse revolts me – vicious spirals of entrapment and fear – the abuser chips away at their victim's self-confidence until they lose their powers of deductive reasoning – rendering themselves a trapped and helpless victim. Innocent mistakes should not be confused with stupid ones. Only life experience provides the layers of understanding required to read dangerous situations ahead of time. There are no instructions to train for the premature loss of innocence or the stark realisation that a lover has a dark side – just manuals for recovery and reconstruction.

Kasia – I recognise your pain. Brutal surface attacks leave side-effects buried deep – but you have to be brave and dig them out. Let me help you – I can show you the way – follow me. When there is a battle ahead – trust me – you want me on your side – loyal to the end. Accepting help is a strength not a weakness. A concept of misplaced pride I have struggled with myself over the years. Kasia, I gave you those phone numbers and as much support as I could in the short time that we had. I know it is so easy when you are on the outside looking in. Kasia, you haven't been back through – I'm worried about you.

"The train now approaching Platform 1 is the 08.07 Southeastern service (blue train) to London Charing Cross calling at West St Leonards, Crowhurst, Battle, Robertsbridge, Etchingham, Stonegate, Wadhurst, Frant, Tunbridge Wells, High Brooms, Tonbridge, and Hildenborough ..."

The Battle of Britain lit up the skies of Kent and the surrounding villages. Hildenborough's close proximity to RAF Biggin Hill meant an emergency landing strip was less than a mile from the village centre. On 6 September 1940, Flying Officer Bowring attacked a

Junkers 88 Bomber. Its radio operator was ordered to bail out and Corporal Agel landed on the roof of the 'Boiling Kettle' tea rooms where he was given tea and cakes by the owners as they waited for the police to arrive. On occasion, the coffee shop provides the same level of service.

'What time is the next train to London?'
'I can't see the board from in here.'
'Which board?'

Chapter 8

Trains of Thought

I LOVE A copy of the Metro. It tells you just enough about what is going on in the world before you lose interest, or more realistically, the time to read any more. I particularly like the Good Deed Feed where people write in with stories about random acts of kindness bestowed on them by strangers. It restores faith in humanity and gives everyone a sense of hope. A kind of 'pay it forward'.

'Rush Hour Crush' – also in the Metro. Romantic proposals from strangers who have caught the eye of another and hope it has been caught back. I'm sure everyone who reads it has a secret hope to see something they believe to be written about them. No? Just me then … Touchingly sentimental love note paragraphs – the first tentative foray into the dating minefield – unless they are invented by a heartless, paid Metro person. I may have turned my back on romance – but that doesn't mean I don't appreciate a bit of romanticism for all the hopefuls out there. May Cupid shoot with alacrity and accuracy (duck) – and at least with his eyes open – otherwise it becomes 'Pin the Tail on the Donkey' – and we've all played that one.

Harriet Harpie Strikes Again

HER VICTIM THIS time was Tatz – bad choice.

"Mum – that bloody woman has been in complaining about everything – I had to make her drink three times, twice with milk, once with soya, too hot, too cold, too weak, too strong – and her kids – oh my God ....
And then she expected a free drink!"
"You mean Harriet Harpie?"
"I can't stand her."
"Me neither."
"Can't you do something?"
"Give her two attempts at a drink and that's her lot."
"Really – can't you just throw her out?"
"Really – and don't swear."

See You Next Tuesday

GHASTLY INDIVIDUALS COME with the territory of offering a service to the public – and I am pleased to say they are in the minority – but when they crawl out from underneath the rocks they are guaranteed to be revolting.

I suffer this particular Sussex Charmer every week, and every week it is the same conversation, with the same outcome. He has a bulldog and he thinks he is a hard man. The dog is ugly, undershot jaw, a very pig of a dog (and I am a dog-lover) and a lookey likey if ever I saw one. He barrels in – usually on a Tuesday – yellow fluorescent vest flapping in the breeze – making him look like 'Angry Bird', or 'Flappy Bird', or 'Yellow Bird' or just a cock.

He adopts a bulldog stance – arms out, chest puffed – ensuring the maximum amount of his revolting body odour is wafted all around the coffee shop. Then comes the Neanderthal grunt – grunt – grunt he says, and it's the same conversation every time – verbatim:

'Do sandwiches?'
'No, only paninis'.
'Why don't you do sandwiches? You're a Cunt.'

Seriously. He says this, then he leaves. I now sell sandwiches – it makes no difference – he just comes in to call me a C …' So, spare me the routine. I look forward to his Tuesday visits immensely.

See You Next Tuesday You C, See You Next Tuesday You C, See you …
I hope never.

'Could I have a large mocha and regular latte with a vanilla shot and a hot chocolate with hazelnut.'

Experimenting with syrup flavourings is another trend standing the test of time – flavours rise and fall according to popularity and the sugar tax.

Menopausal Mary

MENOPAUSAL MARY MADE quite the entrance at the coffee shop today. Gorgeous, stylish, confident and glamorous, she put the fox into silver. I asked her how she was while I made her coffee. She smiled and said *"I? … I am at the top of my game."* And she was today – bold, confident, comfortable, defined and resolute. Unlike last week when I asked her and she bit my head off.

The menopause – isn't that supposed to be the time when old nags are put out to pasture? Don't worry. St Leonard will take care of us all. Mary is in fact magnificent. She made my day and I salute her. She passes through frequently with a charming little dog who is familiar with station etiquette. He does not urinate up the platform signage or worse in the community garden. Don't forget to wash the free produce. She is living proof that you can dazzle at any age. Some of us shine brighter as we get older. I don't worry about age. I am not just saying this because I am getting older. I genuinely don't. I just roll with it – some years I am better than others – but they are in no particular order.

Menopause citations – another burgeoning movement – where women – celebrity or otherwise – are coming out in droves to talk about their experiences – I am mildly disinterested – because they are not telling us anything new – and let's face it – women's cycles – their beginning and their end – are as inevitable for a woman as death. Women are also very good at talking to other women about all things gynaecological – but if you feel the need to shout it from the rafters – then go ahead – could it just not be my rafters during rush hour. In my experience, commuters generally – and men in particular – do not want to hear about cycles with their morning coffee – probably because they are either an inconvenience or an overwhelming relief – depending on the circumstances.

My encounter with Mary did make me think about the passing of time – and how quickly it goes. Mary is sagely carrying with her a wealth of life experience as she strolls casually towards the ranks of society senior. As a child, I remember desperately trying to fast-track my journey into adult hood. I wonder at what point in life do you start viewing Christmas as the probable number of turkeys you have got left to cook in your life-time? For those who fear dying – this may be a frightening calculation and best avoided.

Tea

'What herbal teas do you have?'
Another game with no name. I run through a fairly extensive list
– 'Cherry, camomile, green, peppermint, liquorice, nettle?'
'Forget it, I'll have normal tea with milk – leave the bag in.'
Why does he do this every single time?
It's so tedious – what a wanker.

I should have realised that tea strikes at the very heart of the nation.
It is harder to get it right for people than coffee (thank goodness
Harriet Harpie is a coffee drinker).

'Tea bag in or out?' – Such a critical question of preparation. A
generation ago people were still horrified at the thought of a teabag
– let alone the very suggestion of leaving one floating in a paper cup.
Travel makes bone china and tea strainers redundant – *'recyclable'*
double walled paper cups are the new every-day. Still – it makes for
another amusing coffee shop game (our side) as we make a snap
assessment – gauging who's 'bag in' and who's 'bag out'. Whatever
gets us through the day.

The Loyalty Card

LOYALTY CARDS ARE important – they are symbols of affirmation from
my regular customers. Mutual acknowledgement of reward from
both sides of the counter – the concept of loyalty clearly beyond the
realm of comprehension for the chancer who stole the ink stamper
and a batch of blank cards to counterfeit some completions. Pathetic.

One customer came and strewed an array of my loyalty cards across
the counter. He had discovered them in his desk at the weekend.

Fearful of dying early and having his estate trawl through his valuables – only to discover that he was a man who never cashed his loyalty cards in – he was after some consolidation. I amalgamated and he seemed visibly relieved.

Loyalty is an assessment of personality – a statement of dedication and commitment. To be disloyal should be seen as a betrayal. I am fiercely loyal to friends in my inner circle – it is one of my better qualities. In relationships – like I said – it's a statement of commitment – or not. I am sure my customers have loyalty cards for different coffee shops – that is known as divided loyalty and completely acceptable practice in these circumstances.

This should not be confused with disloyalty – or having your cake and eating it – because that would be unfaithful – something completely different which is unlikely to bring about any kind of consolidation. Deep and meaningful relationships are not normally found working through a cake stand in one sitting – or perhaps they are.

Yes. I have been unfaithful on more than one occasion – but always with the same person – and only when my relationship departure was in the process of being finalised – all physical privileges revoked – along with most verbal communication. This is something I am ambivalent about – because it's done and I cannot change it – nor do I want to – because I love good memories and the sex was amazing for both of us. Maybe it's because whenever we were together, we saw each other as the same teenagers as when we first met – lured back to a more carefree time – without marriage and divorce – children and commitment – financial or otherwise. Or maybe the real magnet was that we actually saw each other – accepting of who we both were – no inhibition – no expectation – no disappointment. Ours was a long course to run. It is always important to finish something on a high note – while I was still forward facing and he was not triangular. We had our swansong on my fiftieth.

While this customer enjoyed his coffee, he confessed that he was old and fearful of dying. In hushed, horrified tones he whispered that he was sixty-five. I laughed out loud. That just is not old. Challenging his numerical fear, I asked him what such an old man was doing on a train to London.

His mantra is Do It Now. Do not delay, do not wait, the time is always now, and he recalled the final words of Sir John Betjeman – at the age of 84 – who said if he had his time again he would definitely have had more sex. I pointed out that he was twenty years away from that number. He smiled – I wonder what he was thinking about?

Tomorrow's too late, tomorrow's too late,

The Polish Courier

SUPPLIERS ARE A law unto themselves – commercial or domestic – everyone has a courier story – usually a bad one – because people only complain or remember invisible people when they give crap service. I have already established that I myself have been quick off the mark to complain in the past – and explained my new strategy of recognition for an otherwise invisible person. If you do not know who they are – it is because they are invisible to you and you should really up your game. I am referring to the people that perform 'menial' but important jobs – toilet cleaners, bin men, ticket sales and coffee shop owners. We have our fair share of customers who see straight through us – dismissive – finger clicking customers. If they come in more than once, we are able to educate them – a simple process – engage them in conversation with a friendly smile – and eventually they are forced to acknowledge the person in front of them. All animals are after all equal – unless they wear a yellow vest and are after a sandwich.

The Polish courier was hard work working hard. He had delivered my coffee since I opened – always sullen, rude and impatient. He never smiled. I sensed a challenge. After all – invisible people should at least be able to see each other – even if the rest of the world is blinkered.

One day, fed up with my friendly greeting being met with resistant indifference, I took a different approach. I took his signing machine from him and turned to sign with my back to him, refusing to turn around. I made a latte, turned around and handed him both – he grinned. Finally, a breakthrough.

He started to talk, told me about his family in Poland and his life in England – where English people are unfriendly. He had come over to work for greater financial opportunity but he missed his family and was finding it difficult to settle. He worked long hours and was paid by the drop, which meant little time for pleasantries anyway.

From that day on he always delivered the coffee with a big smile and asked me how I was. Sometimes he bought a coffee – partial to a shot of vanilla – he joked about how I had forgotten to put it in his latte the first time. The last time I saw him he brought his Polish fiancée to meet me. He had come to say goodbye. A new job with better packages. He said he would always remember the free coffee day – it isn't often anyone does anything nice for him. *"No wonder"*, I said, *"with a face like that."* He found this hilarious. A small victory for me as I wished him good luck – a momentous leap forward for both of us. I know I used to have a face like that – full of belligerence – defiance against the establishment. Ultimately it will get you nowhere – which was probably the intention.

Restoring the Faith

MUSICIANS OF EVERY description come through the coffee shop. I have even seen a small harp on a trolley with an even smaller owner struggling to control it, skateboarding is not permitted on the platform. I was not the only person who breathed a sigh of relief when she wrestled it on to the train. I hope her destination station is stair free.

All in all, it had been a busy but frustrating morning. Technology to blame as usual – the contactless card machine – a commuter's best friend – was not co-operating. I was in the process of re-booting the thing while wishing for a sledgehammer.

This customer was noticeable for his calm, confident demeanour, and his long dreadlocks twisted into a top knot. I was feeling more slip knot. The queue was nearly out of control and everybody's patience was on the back foot. He remained cool and collected. He wanted a deluxe hot chocolate. I groaned inwardly while smiling because it's a faff to prepare and guaranteed to slow down a queue. He also wanted to pay by card. Of course he did – arghhh. I asked him to please take his drink and pay me next time. I wrote the drink off – such is life.

A couple of months later, not long before closing – he walked in through the door saying he owed me some money. I was shocked that he had actually taken the trouble to come back. A reminder to me that the world can be a good place with generous souls and selfish minorities can make us cynical about the majority.

Over another hot chocolate he told me he was a musician and composer. He had to make an unusual choice earlier in life between being a professional track athlete and saxophony.

Ah the saxophone, that dirty instrument remains a thorn in my side. Rejecting the bribe my parents touted – I allowed rebellion to win again and the opportunity was lost. It remains on my list. I asked him if it was too late to learn? He laughed saying it was merely a question of application. Checking his watch his face changed – the witching hour was fast approaching – that time somewhere around 5pm that all parents of small children dread.

"When I walk through the door and my whole family has gone high," he said, *"I go low, real low."* This is possibly the holy grail of family harmony, and a statement that could really only be made by someone with a natural ear for music.

Fortunately for me – life has moved on and 5pm is a sure sign that the sun is approaching the yard arm – I've done my time in the toddler coven.

"We are sorry but the ... service to London Charing Cross has been delayed by 5 minutes. This is due to a signalling fault."

"The train now approaching Platform 1 is the 08.17 Southeastern service (blue train) to London Charing Cross calling at West St Leonards, Crowhurst, Battle, Robertsbridge, Etchingham, Stonegate, Wadhurst, Frant, Tunbridge Wells, High Brooms and Tonbridge ... "

An Act of Parliament passed in 1740 enabled the Medway Navigation company to transport coal and lime into the town and gunpowder, timber and hops to be taken downriver towards the Thames. The town later became famous for Tunbridgeware – finely inlaid wooden boxes and cabinets – sold to 'foils' taking the spa spring water at Royal Tunbridge Wells.

Tannoy Talk

THE TANNOY ANNOUNCEMENTS never say the *'08.17 will now be the 08.22'* – they just focus on the negative. Deflect the disappointment of delay with the positive reinforcement known as hope.

'See it, Say it, Sort it' – THE most boring announcement of them all – deteriorating into a drone as the person recording it clearly loses the will to live. There is serious room for improvement to make these announcements more upbeat and memorable. Good fun could be had and I would be happy to record them myself for free.

I took some time to research train announcements – I know – one step away from Train Spotting! I discovered there is even a forum on the subject. Shoot me now.

The Telegraph even wrote an article about it:

'Husband and wife team Phil Sayer and Elinor Hamilton are the actors whose words were used in thousands of announcements for cancelled trains and delayed services due to "*adverse weather conditions*" … For Mr Sayer, being the voice of trains and tubes has both good and bad sides. The 56-year old former BBC radio presenter and television presenter was thrilled when he was asked to record the iconic "*please mind the gap*" phrase for London's Northern, Piccadilly and Jubilee tube lines.'

His status as the bearer of bad news has also caused him frustration. "*Someone wrote that I sounded smug and conceited giving the announcements … it was quite nasty,"* he said. *"The voice is meant to be a disconnected voice and sound unemotional."*

The tannoy announcements should be put out to tender at the same time as the railway franchises – remember – change is good.

'Large hot chocolate with all the trimmings.'
(Trimmings? It's a beverage not a roast.)

"The train now approaching Platform 1 does not stop here. Trains passing through the station can cause turbulence. Please hold on to push chairs, wheel chairs and old bags."

Dot Cotton

THERE GOES MY skyward eye-roll. When I first met this frail, delicate old lady, I rushed round to the pew to help her. She was sobbing about how she was allergic to every last strand of the clothing on her body. It did cross my mind that if she knew she was allergic then why put it on?

Being in her seventies, I felt she probably wouldn't fabricate such an elaborate story. She sat there all demure and unassuming – sucking me in because I hate to see anyone in genuine distress – unless you are low-life – when I will take a view based on merit.

Dot was tugging frantically at her clothing. I was seriously praying that she wasn't about to take every item off – no nudity in the coffee shop – it is against environmental health regulations. She would not have been the first to strip off in here. Yes, you know who you are. Do not come in here after a yoga class, abusing the pew with your sweaty lycra, as you shamelessly remove everything but your underwear – and that was struggling for pole position – then change into another outfit and eavesdrop on my telephone conversation – before shuffling out without making a purchase. Remember karma!

Fortunately, Dot kept her clothes on – distracted with a coffee – but that too became a drama, too hot, too cold, too much coffee, too much milk, now not enough milk, too small, too big, dropped the lid, gave her another lid – perhaps she had been given a masterclass by Harriet Harpie. Dot put lots of sugars in her bag for later – grateful for my touch of human kindness, and to my relief, caught the train. I grabbed a double espresso.

Dot has been in numerous times now – a different story and profession on each occasion. Dot is needy, uses hushed undertones and makes everything as much of an ordeal for herself as she possibly can. She cannot unscrew her water bottle, sugar a coffee, can only drink hot water, can't open a packet – because Dot likes me to do all these things for her. I used to, until one day I followed her out and caught her ripping open a packet of crisps, swigging her water without a care in the world. All privileges revoked.

Off The Rails

'Are there any toilets at the Station?'
'NO – NO – NO!'
'Why are there no toilets at the Station?'
'Why is the ticket office closed?'

As I have said previously, I have a way of surrounding myself with broken creatives who have a weakness or a vulnerability of some kind. I can focus my attention on fixing them, while hiding behind an invisible smoke screen that shields me from catching sight of my own failings.

As the general public relentlessly make their problems my problems, and behave in ways without manners that can only be described as abnormal – I run the risk of suffering further permanent damage at worst, or malfunctioning at best, as they start to drive me slowly insane. Occupational health or hazard?

Although I joke, there are those with serious mental health problems who feel suicide is the only way out – choosing to fry themselves on the live rail – or obliterate themselves – hitting a train with maximum impact. There was a Samaritans campaign highlighting railway suicides – I hope it was successful.

The coffee shop has opened my eyes to suicide from the other side of the tracks – my side. It was around lunchtime – when I heard a hideous mechanical sound and some screaming. I stayed behind the counter – anxious to avoid the circus.

Stig appeared at the doorway – calm and impressively in control of a dreadful situation.

"So – some woman's just thrown herself under the Victoria train and we are closing the Station." I rushed out to grab the signs in – the train had stopped just past booking hall. Police and ambulances were arriving on the scene – I was one more person in the way – so I hurried to shut the shop up as quickly as possible. I felt sorry for the driver. Disgustingly, people on the far embankment seemed to be taking photos on their phone.

Stig came back – *"Seems she's alive – she's managed to miss the live rail – got in between the rails and the train hasn't mangled her…"* – no drama from him – just a bullet-point factual account. I exited the side gate as quickly as possible feeling a bit sick.

Suicides on train tracks are a frequent occurrence – I believe there was one the same afternoon – same line – bit further up – they were successful – or not – depending on how you view life.

Breaking and Entering

MY DAY STARTS at 4.30 am – a supplier had missed my delivery. I had to do a Saturday night stock drop at the shop otherwise Roberto would be on my case first thing. Delivery driver, director of refuse, packhorse – all part of my job description – somewhere along the road I had dropped my sense of humour. I try to avoid St Leonards at night, the dynamics typically change after dark.

The platform was packed as I negotiated my way through, balancing stock, handbag and keys. I put the key in the lock – it snapped off – wedged inside the lock. Swearing at the door, I felt a sudden rise of anger and was ready to explode. I attempted to remain calm, determined to help myself.

Imagine the scene – the platform is packed – I had already caused a minor drama at the door. I now decided to jump-kick the lock in. Confident that my years of body combat classes would stand me in good stead – I let fly. I only jarred my back a little bit. The door held fast and nobody on the platform even gave me a second glance. I am fairly confident that somebody on the platform would know how to get me into the unit in record time – no-one was forthcoming.

Time to up the ante at home. Certain tones have different meanings – my children recognise this. I phoned my eldest son, Seb, with my 'do not mess with me tone' – code for I am borderline hysterical and panicking and need you to get me out of the shit. My son is practical – a logical thinker in adverse situations. He decided not to laugh at my plight – much – and assured me he was on his way.

You cannot miss him at 6ft 7. A super-fit rower with a commanding presence – particularly when wearing a black beanie, black gloves and carrying a bag full of tools – all ready to do a job on a Saturday night. He methodically laid the tools out on the platform bench. Still nobody questioned it. Not one raised eyebrow to indicate a modicum of public awareness. This is obviously completely normal Saturday night behaviour at St Leonards.

To his credit, my son managed to remove the broken key. As we were contemplating whether he should kick the door in, Tatz turned up with her now ex-boyfriend. He took out his credit card and flipped open the lock. I hate having to feel grateful to an arsehole! The door flung open and we all piled in. There was no hearty cheer from the platform – because they pretended never to see a thing – I suspect they were not even pretending.

See It, Say It, Sort It? Fat chance.

Sheik Yerbouti

THIS MAN BOTHERS me – not because I think he is a terrorist, or trying to make a big political statement or a danger to the public. He bothers me because he is a complete twat.

He loiters in or just outside the coffee shop. He never buys anything nor do I want him to. I just want him to go away – far away. He wears a red chequered tea towel on his head – often with the label showing saying polyester – secured with a black curtain tie-back with an exaggerated tassel. If this is a nod to an Arabian head dress – it is abysmal and embarrassing. He wears flip flops, whatever the weather, and cotton trousers – rolled up over his calves – his huge belly spills over his belt – which struggles valiantly to support both flab and trousers. His shirt buttons strain, finding themselves permanently under pressure.

So, there he is – an absolute picture of loveliness. St Leonards very own Sheik Yerbouti. He then chants in a mysterious language while hopping from foot to foot. This is either a ritualistic kind of dance to accompany his chanting – or he is another victim of the lack of toilet facility. Personally, I think it is all part of his act. He carries a rucksack – who knows why and who cares. On reflection, I have it on good authority that once on the train – always a blue train – he heads straight for the toilet – so perhaps it is a combination of dance and drainage.

He is not mentally incapacitated – just deliberately trying to be offensive. I have heard him have a rational, and I use the word in its loosest sense, conversation with someone who had the pleasure of standing next to him on the platform – perhaps they were acquainted.

Why does he insist on hopping from foot to foot directly in front of the coffee shop? If he could just grapevine to the right or to the left – he would be out of my line of vision and my day would improve instantaneously. Mind the gap!

To the left, to the right, to the left, to the right and grapevine.

'Toilets?'
'Sorry no.'
'You are fucking kidding me.'
'No.'

Sanctuary of the Potting Shed

THIS IS MY favourite oasis of calm – tucked far away from the madding crowds. I become the anonymous public and am afforded 'regular' recognition status. I love the Potting Shed and go there for very late lunches – or cake. Sometimes I meet a friend and we put her world or mine to rights over coffee and cake, an excellent German tradition. Other times I go there by myself to reflect. Time in my own head space is priceless – I need it – shutting out the chatter of day to day. My most creative time is 5am – walking through the woods in the middle of nowhere with dogs and nature – allowing thoughts to ramble on through my mind. Driving loud and fast helps me think about specifics.

I don't always feel like speaking about myself. I can be a private person – hard to read – and it can be even harder to interpret what I say – possibly and maybe – my default sentence prefixes. I seldom seek counsel over the things that are really bothering me. Perhaps I should. I know I am not an easy person to be in a relationship with. I can talk to hundreds of strangers about anything and everything – but when it comes to confiding in a partner – I tend to have nothing relevant to say. I wonder why that is? I expect, if I could really be arsed to psycho-analyse myself, there are conclusive case studies somewhere that will neatly relate it all back to trust, commitment and sex. Tediously dull. I am not commitment phobic – I just don't want to feel emotionally and physical trapped – and anyway – I can't be a phobic – because relationships aside – I commit all the time – happy to dive straight in. I do not fear relationships. I am not scared of anything. I always tackle adversity head on to ensures the hit is square – but not necessarily fair.

The Potting Shed coffee is not as good as ours – obviously – inter-coffee-shop snobbery – or coffee brand loyalty? But when someone brings you a cup on a tray that you haven't had to make or clear away – somewhere nearer the end of a very long day – all you feel is gratitude.

This particular day I felt oddly empty. I ordered a cortado – yes really – they are my favourite – if they are made correctly. My life is so busy – surrounded by people at work, surrounded by teenagers at home. I am always on the go for one reason or another. As I sat quietly, reflecting into my coffee, I had an unwelcome and unfamiliar sensation of loneliness and felt a sudden wave of wanting to belong – to someone rather than something. Was it too late?

I have had several marriage proposals in my life – before and after my marriage – and I always found a way to ensure I inadvertently (fucked off at break neck speed – usually up a mountain – without a backward glance – and no offer of an explanation) dodged them. I have no regrets – and certainly never had a desire to start a collection of unwanted engagement rings. I buy my own jewellery. I like it better this way as it is commitment free and goes with anything.

I finished my coffee and came to the conclusion that belonging to someone was overrated. After all, it's not like I never had my chances and I decided every time to go it alone. Part of me genuinely wants a long-term, permanent, serious connection. But I seem to prefer relationships that are non-committal – which is probably why it worked so well with Ian. I know how not to belong.

I also knew deep down that I missed Station Man more than I wanted to admit – so I won't – instead I will do what I always do – whack a plaster over it to prevent any unsavoury seeping – and move on.

"The train now approaching platform 1 is the 12.42 Southern service (green train) to Brighton calling at Bexhill, Collington, Cooden Beach,

Normans Bay, Pevensey Bay, Pevensey and Westham, Hampden Park, Polegate and Eastbourne ... "

The sunshine coast – apparently – and the retirement capital of Sussex. Beachy Head nearby – a hot spot of its own for suicide attempts and successes. Some are prevented – similar to the railway. Mind the gap. Eastbourne – a larger shit-hole further up the coast – also holds the record for the most people crammed into both a mini – and the two-carriage green train to Brighton on a Saturday morning.

Chapter 9

Park Life

THERE WAS A distinct nip in the air when an American day-time regular called in for her alternative milk latte – toddler son strapped safely in the pushchair – much to his disgust. He amused himself throwing his hat and gloves across the coffee shop. She amused me as she kept picking them up and putting them back on him – classic cause and effect. Toddlers can't be patient. I respect impatience. I hurried up.

She was frustrated as the weather was turning and soon it would be too cold for him to play outside. This was probably their last park day.

Too cold? I thought she was joking. I lived in snowy Colorado with my three children all aged under 3 – I can get park suits on toddlers in record-breaking time – because the alternative is to stay cooped up at home – climbing the walls looking for my mind.

I gave her the benefit of my parenting experience – keep taking him outside. Boys are different to girls, there is no point pretending otherwise. I have both. Like dogs, boys need fresh air and wide-open spaces before they can settle indoors. Girls are more adaptable.

My advice was not well received. She became haughty and enlightened me with some parenting advice of her own – she preferred *not* to bring gender differentiation into his life. Oh please – here comes a whole new trend where you are guaranteed to say the wrong thing and completely piss someone off for having a contrary opinion. Oh look – snowflakes! Don't say that looking down your nose at me. At least have the conversation. I think we have long accepted that there are different genitalia. You can have one or the other or you can change – be whoever you want to be and I will be happy for you. Could somebody please come up with a better name than gender fluidity – as the fluid part correlates directly back to genitalia and tissues – which I do not sell in the shop.

I smiled politely, and she left me with a vision of herself – climbing the politically correct walls of winter, searching for gender neutrality.

Motherhood takes us all by surprise. It is impossible to prepare for, but once it is here, there should be no turning back. It is a life-long commitment and if done properly, it is not for the faint hearted. I never thought I would have children. I avoided prams and you would never find me cooing over somebody's little bundle of joy – unless it had paws, fur and a wagging tail. It wasn't a conscious thing – I just was not interested. Fortunately, it is very different when you have your own. Maternal instinct is incredibly powerful for a reason.

Being a good mother is a never-ending journey – bringing with it a whole new dimension and definition to life – for better and for worse. No journey worth taking is ever smooth. For me, motherhood made me a better person. It taught me how to learn patience and how to make unconditional personal sacrifices. My children have a slightly different view – and have screamed 'you are such a crap mother' at me on numerous occasions. I expect I am sometimes – because when they all kick off – it is enough to drive a person to the downstairs loo with a large glass of merlot! Parenting effectively can be a challenge – one I believe I have risen to successfully – because my children are all successful – they have their own sense of purpose and what constitutes achievement to them as individuals. Motherhood brings a unique set of rewards. I accept it has grounded me for now. I also appreciate it is not for everyone.

I now know this regular a little better. She has a good sense of humour. A typical mother, juggling many balls while putting her son's needs before her own. She was in the process of reinventing her career – training to be a counsellor for troubled, angry teenagers. I smile inwardly – I could have been a case study. At St Leonards, some of our weakest members are the children – adult life forced on them by vacating parents – who either couldn't be arsed, or were never equipped to see the job through. Or children having children – emotionally and financially unable to care for the contents of a pram – ensuring a steady supply of troubled teenagers desperately in need of support – but too reluctant to conform to a level that will allow them to accept any. This community needs her to complete her training.

I acknowledge that we are all very precious about our first child – and sometimes I should keep my opinions to myself as they are not always welcome or relevant.

The Angel

THIS HAD BEEN going on for some weeks in the run up to Christmas and was getting mildly irritating. A Christian lady would come in, purchase a coffee, then help herself to a large handful of wooden stirrers which she shoved in her bag. So far, I had let it go. This time I gave her a steely-eyed look of disapproval. She immediately knew why (guilty?) – and announced indignantly that she needed the stirrers for her craft project. I left it there.

I am running a business and cannot just give everything away to everybody – the business has overheads – surely everyone understands this basic fact of business economics? Bottom lines have a bad habit of fluctuating – unless you sit on them – as their name advises you to do. This is why you now have to ask for napkins and sweeteners. I have no objection to supplying either for my paying customers. I do resent people taking entire pots of sweetener – because it is a relatively expensive product – and I also decline the opportunity to supply the whole of the Station with free tissues because it's cold and their noses are running. I am not a charity – all those that know me know I do my share on the freebie front.

'Can I have a cup of water?' – a frequent demand from non-paying customers – and espresso drinkers. The cups I use are relatively expensive and I get hundreds of requests. The water is free – the cups are not. I have implemented a new system. If you are happy to pay for your cup – I am happy to fill it with water, provided you put the money in one of the charity boxes – you choose – RNLI or MRI.

One day a red-faced, dirty, track suit asked for water. He didn't have any money for a cup and instead of giving me a mouthful of bad language while demanding something for nothing, he went and sat quietly outside. I can be a soft touch and he was clearly in need. I took him some water. He was grateful and welcome because he was nothing but polite and even put his cup in the bin when his train pulled in. A reminder to me of the importance of the milk – or water – of human kindness.

I'm glad I relented and the minority arseholes haven't stopped me being kind. The Station will always help passengers who require water anyway – no need for a mirage situation.

Shortly before Christmas, the Christian came in again, purchased a coffee and presented me with a hand knitted Christmas decoration. A white, woollen angel complete with gold halo, glued to one of my coffee stirrers.

She explained that she had been making them for the local church. Another customer admired the angel decoration and asked if she could buy some. Her turn for the steely look – *"Angels are not for sale – gifts only!"* – then she turned on her heel and walked out.

The coffee shop does not embrace the 'Deck the Halls' approach to Christmas. The Booking Hall has it covered – they have a tree and a Christmas Train light stuck in the ticket office window. We opt out because we respect all religious beliefs, are shut between Christmas and New Year – because time with family is important – which in turn makes us all look forward to January – and because I am sick of seeing Christmas decorations from August onwards.

I am not a religious person. I was shown the Church of England by my parents. We went to church every Sunday until we were allowed to decide for ourselves. Fortunately, the Vicar looked like John Travolta, so the hour passed relatively quickly. The velvet collection bag always confused me – was it guilt money or protection money? I was surprised to discover in my mid-teens that my father was actually a Quaker. It is quite brave parenting to have a faith that you feel very strongly about but refuse to impose on your children. This allows them the freedom to become and believe what they feel is right for them.

I will visit old churches and cathedrals if I am somewhere interesting and the mood takes me. I find stained glass windows fascinatingly beautiful even though churches sometimes smell like a florist. Otherwise, my church going habits are reserved for funerals rather than weddings. Darwin made far more of an impression on me than the Gardens of Eden.

The tannoy joins in the festive fun in September – 'Ho Ho Ho Merry Christmas …' and then goes on to explain that it is not Christmas, and there is nothing to be jolly about when it is Christmas – because all the trains will be disrupted due to planned engineering works.

Roberto hated the woollen Angel. I keep her under the counter where she remains like a little talisman. Her maker had not been in for months and months. December came around again and I resurrected the Angel – giving her pride of place behind the wall socket just below the menu board. As I turned around, in she walked, asking for a large latte. The timing gave me goose bumps. I glanced up apprehensively but no lightning bolt was evident.

'Can I have a small black coffee with no milk?'
'Is your coffee fairly strong?'
'Yes.'
'In which case – top it up with cold water.'
'Somebody save me.'

Stock Control

A DIFFICULT SKILL to master as factors become variables. Getting stock control right is crucial to my business. I never know how many customers will come through on any given day. I do know that the weather plays a part, and delays that cause havoc with trains can have an immediate impact on stock. Excess orders go out of date – wasted. Insufficient stock looks bad and loses potential sales.

I must mention the Polish Courier's replacement here. He bravely managed to deliver the coffee on the one snowy, icy, gridlock day of the year. Carnage on the roads. I had got down to St Leonards OK, but all roads out are up hill. I wondered what the pew would be like to sleep on. Adding to the misery of the day – the booking office was closed. People were seeking refuge in the shop – hot chocolate sales were up – and for the old economics formula of supply and demand to work – to make lots of hot chocolate – you need lots of milk.

The weather meant I had not been able to do the milk run that morning – supplies were dwindling fast. Normally I can shoot up the road and grab some – but the shop was wall to wall with desperate travellers. Chucking them on to the platform would have been heartless.

Hail the new delivery man. He struggled down the platform with the delivery just as I sold my last latte and the milk ran out. Time to make a fair trade. A free latte in exchange for him doing the milk run? Worth a shot.

The power of coffee as a call to action is impressive. Realising this was the only way he was going to get his latte – and realising I was in the shit – he took the money I gave him – enough for 24 pints of milk – and he trudged back out across the tundra. Shortly afterwards he returned with 2 pints and change, saying I had given him far too much money. I made him a coffee and got my coat on.

Struggling back with the missing 22 pints, I recalled a maths problem I had seen, printed as a joke in a national newspaper. *"If I throw a triangle out of the car and the car is going 20 mph and wind resistance is a thing that exists, how many cupcakes can Pedro buy with one human soul..."* Pedro – I feel your pain.

"Delayed 30 minutes or more?"
"It is easy to get your money back."
"Simply apply for Delay Repay online at Southeastern railway.co.uk/ delay-repay."
"Hassle-free refunds the way they should be." Apparently and unlikely.

Testicular Bells

The platform was packed with families – trains were cancelled – tempers were fraying. Passengers were taking it in turns to swear at the disabled toilet door in the booking hall. I wanted to use the toilet and sneaked through – signalling discretely to Stig to let me in to the office. Comfort breaks have to be timed between trains and never during rush hour – we just have to foot hop until the 09.32 has departed.

As I weaved my way back through the crowded platform I saw Rosie outside the coffee shop. Oh my goodness, what was he wearing and what was he doing? Dressed in the most miniscule leather skirt, fishnet stockings, spikey heels and a basque that deliberately didn't cover his nipples. This was clearly a deliberately provocative attempt at al fresco burlesque. He was singing very loudly and very badly – forcing everyone to look in his direction. He seemed to be performing an aerobic workout at the same time. To the left – to the right – a few bicep curls – a few hamstring curls. To my horror, I realised his skirt was far too short to cover his credentials – which were swinging in the breeze for all to see. As I approached, I raised my finger as a warning.

"ROSIE – don't you dare grapevine!"

A platform observer asked me if Rosie was on something – possibly a redundant question. I bumped into him one day on the walk between Covent Garden and Charing Cross. It can be awkward when you see your customers out of context – particularly when they catch me in somebody else's coffee shop. Rosie was teetering down the street in the highest of heels – somewhat dishevelled and his hair was not quite on straight. I gave him a friendly smile to acknowledge our connection.

"You can fuck off", was his reply – in his best Gloucester of course.

I burst out laughing – how arrogant of me to think I feature as relevant anywhere other than behind my counter where I belong – because I am invisible.

The Ice Queen

NEVER JUDGE A book by its cover, even though it is much harder not to. I think we are all guilty of making an assumption about someone based on a first impression. Is that an assumption or a judgement?

Years ago, I worked for Mark Brown – management consultant/ author – he had devised a training package called 'The Bigot's Pack' – probably obsolete now. It contained a series of images of train passengers and asked you to make a judgment about them – the whole point being not to make a judgment at all. He was a minority pin stripe.

The Ice Queen had been in several times. Striking earrings, enviable style and educated manner. Quietly authoritative, never chatty, never rude – but always distant. One day she had a valid complaint. Constructive criticism is of course welcome.

Actually, it's not really welcome, is it? You have to politely suck it up. I place constructive criticism on the Rooibos tea shelf – to the back on the far left – right next to the customer comment cards inside the customer suggestion box – that I do not in fact have. This is because I find them cowardly. I hope that if you have a comment to make you will tell me – like the Ice Queen!

I admit that I am somewhat sensitive to criticism. I also know I am defensive about being defensive. I don't need to be told. See? – defend! When direct criticism strikes I find it hard to deal with – I frantically try to defend myself, usually with an offensive counter-strike or a clever defensive manoeuvre. This is not because I have to be right about everything – if only it were that simple. I just can't cope with being wrong – with the emphasis on 'I'. In my head, they are two different scenarios. I know – it's a problem. Criticism, constructive or otherwise, is a negative judgment – which subconsciously reminds us of feeling inadequate when criticised as a child. I wish I had understood this at the beginning of the parenting ladder. I remember being told by a primary school teacher that I had a black streak in me. I was 6. I still remember it. I presume it wasn't a compliment.

I appreciate criticism could actually be beneficial to the business. I therefore have to learn to take it on the chin, even though this cuts my core. I am my own harshest critic and could lead a master class in self-criticism. My bar for personal performance is set so high that when someone points out a fundamental flaw, I am angry with myself, because I should have realised it long before anyone needed to highlight its existence. I may have to accept that perfection is a destination I will never reach – this doesn't stop me trying. I wish I could be one of those people who genuinely laugh things off. I am not.

The Ice Queen's complaint was the naked exposure of the pastries to customer violation – particularly the person who had sneezed forcefully all over them yesterday – on a day when a very temporary member of staff was behind the counter. Roberto would never have allowed it. Disgusting. I know I would have complained myself. The pastries come in fresh every day and are normally gone very quickly. Her criticism upheld – and in the interest of food hygiene, the pastries are now individually bagged – as they should have been from the outset. Mea bloody culpa! I can beat myself up about this every time I look at them.

The ice started to soften with this simple change in display, and I realised that 'Pastrygate' went much deeper than a couple of croissants. At the coffee shop, connections must be quick and people make snap decisions. I have little room for negotiation error. Orders have to be right and interactions positive. Of course, there are exceptions and failings on both sides – I have already admitted I sometimes get it wrong. The coffee shop is there to serve. Good coffee makes people feel better. I like to make people feel better – they have a great start to the day and I can spend the day feeling good about myself – the best kind of exchange.

This customer was a well-known author who lived locally. Here was a perfect opportunity for a social experiment – a coffee shop version of Hobson's Choice – a free choice when only one thing is offered – take it or leave it. I offered to sell her book, commission free, and only her book. I positioned it on the counter amongst the muffins. I sold a considerable number of copies for one tiny coffee shop. Interesting. Maybe we all expect too much choice. I provide an extensive snack range to cater for everyone because this is what is expected. In theory, the Hobson principle should also apply to snack choices. I'm not quite brave enough to implement it.

'Teabag in or out?'
'One in and one out – lots of milk.'
'Put the sugar in for me love.'
'I will put the sugar in for you love, if I do not have a queue out of the door love, and if I do love, you will have to do it yourself, love!'
'Don't you like being called love?'

The Pirate

FAR MORE JOHNNY Rotten and English Channel than Johnny Depp and the Caribbean – but a pirate all the same. He has a 'pieces of eight' sized hoop in his ear. I'm sure I've seen a bandana about his person, and if pirates are his bag, he is in the right town. Another Londoner lured here by the low rents. He is a London Underground train driver and comes in now and again for a large tea, chocolate dunkers and a big chat on his way to a late shift. He always voices his political views loudly.

Don't discuss religion or politics in the shop – not censorship – it's just not going to well unless everybody is in agreement. The coffee shop counter is not the right forum. If you sit on the pew – all prayers must remain inward. It is for the best. This is the voice of experience.

The Pirate likes a good moan – it's the Brit in him. He also likes to do card tricks on my counter which I never have the time or the inclination to watch. Sometimes I get trapped behind the counter which causes politeness cramps in my legs.

He is a serious cat lover – I am not. He adopted a rescue cat and was devastated early on in their bonding days to find she had escaped, probably running for the tunnel to save herself from the card-trick repertoire. He feared she was a goner. He could hardly contain his excitement next time he came in – grinning from one pieces of eight to the other. The Ship's Cat was alive and well – albeit without a ship. I was pleased for him – ignoring the sinking feeling I was getting with the realisation that I would have to hear the story ad infinitum. I tried to play patience in the hope of finding some by focusing on its happy ending.

The last time I saw him he was rather shaken. Please don't let this be another cat drama. Not this time. He'd been working a late shift in London and was walking across a darkly lit car park when a gang threw a bottle of liquid over him. He was terrified that it was acid, but was so relieved when it turned out to be urine.

It is a sad state of affairs when a pirate is grateful that somebody has thrown urine over him. What happened to civilisation? I doubt the urine-tossers can spell it, even if they have heard of it. I hope they are charged at the very least with urinating in a public place. Speaking of urination – the end of the building on Platform 1 nearest to the Bo Peep tunnel is still station property – not – I repeat not – a public convenience – even though it now smells like one. The tannoy really needs to expand its repertoire.

'Can I have a large mocha to take out please and a sausage roll. Do you have any napkins?'
'Can I have a bottle of water at room temperature please?'

This always amuses me because room temperature for me is either Sahara Midday or Arctic Baltic, when the water could well be warmer in the chiller. I smile and oblige.

"The train now approaching Platform 1 is the 08.50 Southeastern service (blue train) to London Charing Cross calling at West St Leonards,

Crowhurst, Battle, Robertsbridge, Etchingham, Stonegate, Wadhurst, Frant, and Tunbridge Wells … And High Brooms"

Royal Tunbridge Wells – a pretentious town in Kent. In 1606 a courtier to James 1 was staying in Eridge at a hunting lodge. He hoped the country air would improve his ill health and discovered a chalybeate (iron-rich) spring. His health improved when he drank from the spring – establishing it as a spa retreat – a favourite past-time for head foils.

Chapter 10

Behind Closed Doors

I HAVE ALWAYS preferred natural light. On the odd occasion – like this one – when the glare from the general public or the overhead strip lighting has simply done me in – I feel the need to switch the lights off. This is a precautionary measure to instil calm and deflect a possible headache. On these occasions, I am best unprovoked. I do my level crossing best to be on good form, but my work ethic means I'll have an off day when I should probably have a day off instead. I have had to learn the importance of rest. Sometimes I snap and am immediately sorry.

'Coffee love please. Blimey its dark in here – times hard? Saving electric or didn't you pay the bill?'
'Not afraid of the dark then – I can hardly see you.'
'Shame I can see you.'
'Alright love – Jesus.'
'I'm sorry – bad day'
'That's alright love – we all have them – hope your day gets better.'

Life was bothering me – always there for others in a supporting role – wishing someone was there doing the same for me. It was a grey day anyway – my head was rumbling, thoughts of Station Man were oozing out from under the plaster. I had fronted out most of the morning shift, keeping it together, business as usual, but I was becoming more accepting of the fact that my heart had taken a possible battering. I have arranged my life so that I am too busy to pay attention to these matters. Around 11.30 am the Station quietens down – all commuters safely despatched through Bo Peep to take on their own problems. I sat down on the stool behind the till – trying to assemble my thoughts back into their own compartments.

"Hello Gorgeous." In walked one of my favourite customer's – one of my very first in fact. We've had many a conversation about everything and nothing, before he jumps on his train. Sometimes slightly longer ones where he missed it talking to me.

"Knowing what I know about women and walking in to that look – I should walk back out and not return for at least a couple of hours."

Appreciating his effort, I gave him a half-smile and turned to make his latte – hoping to gain composure by gripping the coffee handle hard. I didn't fool him – and I got defensive with his gentle interrogation. I couldn't tell him what was wrong because to speak it out loud would mean having to accept it. I was pacing the front line. I do this when I am formulating a solution to a problem or planning an exit strategy. He was looking straight at me. His eyes enquired but his gaze had me in his sight. Without warning, he took control of the situation and turned to lock the coffee shop door. Just him and me now. A bold move – I respect bold moves. The counter remained between us – but he leaned over and took my arm – I flashed my eyes at him – a warning or a challenge – he could decide.

"Shall we just not work today – go out and get pissed – see where the road takes us?" – I said.

"I can't do that – because I wouldn't trust myself" – was his reply.
"Trust? Who said anything about trust?" – the challenge was issued.

His eyes betrayed him. Slowly and deliberately he walked around to my side of the counter and put his arms around me – deadlock or check mate? Compassion is virtuous – desire is a sinner. The mood was tantalizingly dangerous. Defiance is an inevitable game changer.

Cause A Rebellion

IN MY OWN way, I was testing him. He is always conformist. He has confined himself to his own navy straitjacket of politically correct procedure. That is his choice – but his eyes expose him. I prefer to walk on the wild side – it is a lot more fun, more edgy, more exhilarating. It's all a game anyway. I knew what he wanted and so did he. There was no need for a code – it was written all over his face. He used to have a rebellious nature but traded it in for rules and regulations. If you don't want to rebel then don't stand there stroking my arm telling me how much you care about me. Don't get hold of me if you are scared to go the distance – because on a bad day with a sidewise grin – I might take both of us for a ride – make sure you understand the pros and cons of hitchhiking.

I understand he doesn't like me in the way that he thinks he wants to – although what he fantasises about is up to him. What he does have is admiration – but he prefers to admire me from the safety of the other side of the counter. He admires my achievement, my guts, my determination to see anything through. He knows I am a good listener, he is too. I am a problem solver, creative thinker – a kind, caring, loyal, confident, proud, stubborn, headstrong, impatient, hot headed, passionate, fiery woman with an unnerving ability to blow ice when I need to. Welcome to my game face.

This is what he thought he wanted to handle – but one moment of hesitation opens the floodgate for weakness to seep in. For me, weakness always reverses attraction. He reminded me of other men in my life – impersonating strong powerful protectors – while trying to get off on my strength – feeding off it like helpless parasites. I find this distasteful. I stepped over the gauntlet of challenge. On that particular day, he didn't have the balls I needed to see it through. There may be other days.

We retrieved ourselves to our respective positions of safety. Finding his way back to the public side, he bent down to retrieve his halo from the floor, unlocked the door and shook his head. *"This kind of thing doesn't happen in real life"*, he said, *"particularly on a Tuesday"*.

Except it did happen, one particular Tuesday. No regrets – either side of the counter. The memory treasured – a sweetener to use on days that are tart.

"The train now approaching platform 1 was about to take him away. Sometimes I hate that train."

'Do sandwiches?'
'No, only paninis'.
'Why don't you do sandwiches? You're a C ....'

Guilty Pleasure

'Alright darling? Large tea lots of milk, bag out and some chocolate – I need it today – exhausted – been slapping on tickets everywhere.'

On our first meeting, I thought he was going to be a grumpy sod

– but he actually had a heart of gold. Somewhat on the grandfatherly, large side, always in a Hi-Viz vest that stood no chance of doing up. He usually appeared around lunch-time. He'd been coming in for several months before he confessed that I was his guilty pleasure and how irritated he gets when he comes in and finds that 'bloody foreign bloke' behind the counter.

Meet: The Car Park Patrol Man!

He had begun his working life in the army and had witnessed much unpleasantness in his line of duty, which was why he said he took 14 sugars in his tea. He mentioned Lent as an opportunity for change – I assumed he would give up sugar – but instead he opted to stop making air-fix models until Easter. He said this would be very challenging as he was unsure what to do with his hands of an evening. I decided against venturing down that line of enquiry.

Car Park Patrol Man was plagued by plantar fasciitis from too much portly, hot footing it around station car parks up and down the Southeastern line, rushing to get tickets issued before owners returned. It was a sales job – he had a target to meet – with that in common – we formed a connection. Ticket issues worked on a bonus system for him – hence the incentive. He has since transferred to a sedentary position in Kent.

I always used to give him a discount which he put straight in the Lifeboat Collection Tin – I love a swing and a roundabout. That tin will miss him. So do I – even though he always tried to look down my top.

"The train now approaching platform 1 is the 12.10 Southern service (green train) to Brighton calling at Bexhill, Eastbourne, Polegate and Lewes ..."

Lewes is famous for radicalism, Harveys Brewery, Prison, Bonfire and the execution of protestant martyrs. Lewes is Sussex's salvation for all those in exile from Oxfordshire.

Unattended Baggage

ADOPTION IS A surprisingly frequent topic of conversation across the counter – those that are, those that wish they were, those that are about to be, those that never should have been in the position to make a monumental decision about another person's future. Antisocial services. I do not trust them – I believe their decisions could benefit from an injection of personal experience. Perhaps it should become a new requisite for the job.

I am adopted – something I have always known. I always knew I would trace my birth mother when I was finally comfortable with who I am – it is important not to try and back-fill a void. I wanted validation of the sense of belonging, along with the missing pieces of my puzzle. Forty proved to be the right time for me.

I had to go to social services to get my original name. It was December and my name proved to be a festive one – no not Santa. I pointed this out to antisocial services who reprimanded me for not taking the process seriously. Process? Do me a favour. They had no idea. They suggested I read the adopted person's Bible – Primal Wound – they thought it might help me. I glowered as I stalked out. I still haven't read it. A close friend, also adopted, recently leant it to me to read. It remains face down by my bed. Perhaps I should turn it over – perhaps I already know what it says.

My mother is a remarkable woman who I lovingly refer to as The Squadron Leader (just not to her face). She is the woman who elected to claim me as her own and invest her whole life into making mine better. We clashed a lot when I was growing up. I blamed her for everything, for which I apologise. My childhood was happy and enriched. I was fortunate enough to have been re-homed with intelligent, educated, long haul parents who selflessly understood the needs of a child. I am sure there are numerous occasions when they would cheerfully have handed me back!

I met my biological mother one surreal day. She seemed familiar or maybe I wanted her to be. I gave her an opportunity to tell her story. I felt detached during our meeting and an overwhelming desire to get as far away from her as possible. I realised I didn't need her – I certainly had no wish to belong to her. I cross-referenced her story back through my social services file – archived in Berkshire – re-directed to Sussex. Her story was a lie – how pathetically predictable. I retreated into the shadows of anonymity. In my file, a social worker had written in the notes that she feared for my adoption chances because I was such an ugly baby. How rude. Perhaps I grinned sideways on selection day.

Our meeting did raise the loaded question of nature or nurture? I have always had an interest in Law – and once thought seriously about joining the Police. Is this because my (adopted) father was a magistrate – or is it because biologically I come from a long line of Reading CID?

Does my passion for nature come from all the rambles I went on growing up – or from being left as a baby at the bottom of a garden in a pram day and night by my foster carer who suffered from depression? Was it during those early weeks – excluded in the cold and the dark with no sense of belonging – that I learnt how to become a fighter?

She loves me, she loves me not …

"Please do not leave your luggage unattended on the station. Luggage left unattended may be removed without warning or placed up for adoption."

Object Constancy

THIS IS THE concept that even when we cannot see someone – they do not fundamentally change. Very early in life we develop an internalised image of our parents – feeling safe in the knowledge that we are still loved – even when we cannot physically see them. This concept shatters with trauma – such as being abandoned at birth by your mother – the one person who should be pre-programmed to always be there for you. The legacy left to all adopted children is a subconscious fear of abandonment. We go through life feeling insecure and unworthy of love – struggling with the concepts of trust, commitment and emotional intimacy. Struggling with the concepts …. Oh … shit.

"My mother doesn't understand me." Does yours? Will my children say this about me? I expect they already do. Men never say this about their fathers – I wonder why? Probably because we don't expect them to – or because they don't stop to think about it. Mothers are supposed to be understanding of everyone, hence the sense of huge disappointment when we realise that our own does not understand us at all. Just be happy if they stayed the distance.

'Can you tell me which train I need to get for Eastbourne?'
'It's the Southern service from this platform.'
'Ok – can I have a cappuccino then?'
'Chocolate on top?'
'Go on then. Sorry which train?'

'The green one. Coming now.'
'Oh. Where's it going to?'
'Eastbourne ...'

Primal Pain

LIKE I SAID, adoption is a surprisingly common topic over the counter – almost as if we seek each other out – or recognise a trait – or a traitor. Jack rushed in through the door pushing a baby-empty pram packed full of bags and in need of a large latte. Nothing unusual about him, early seventies – tanned with a white goatee – and quite charming. I asked him where he was heading. He was on his way to St Thomas's Hospital to see his baby granddaughter who was fighting for her life. I wished her well – he just made his train.

As his tiny granddaughter put up a brave fight – he became a regular. I witnessed the emotional strain taking its toll. He and his wife were both retired, and legal guardians, not only to her but to their other young granddaughter, and had been since their birth. His step daughter was married to heroin and alcohol and now Jack was bent over with worry about securing a future for the little ones. He was struggling with the thought of putting the little girls up for adoption.

I asked why he was even considering it when he cared so much about them. His eyes misted up as he explained he and his wife would probably die around the time the girls were in Junior school, which would leave them bereaved with huge abandonment issues to overcome. Adoption was the better solution. Quietly, I told him that adoption would leave them with huge abandonment issues too. He looked me square in the eye and told me he knew only too well.

Jack was born in Northern Ireland. His mother died of tuberculosis contracted from drinking milk from the cow pail when he was six. His father, left with a farm and numerous children, put him in an orphanage, where as the only Catholic boy there, he was segregated from the Protestant children. The 'Church' was supposed to pay for his keep but frequently forgot. Matron – I braced myself for a horror story about Magdalena abuse – but to my relief Matron loved him and always piled his food plate high – *"far more than the Proddy boys got"* – he grinned as he told me. The orphanage toilets fascinated him – they were in a line of steps – height ascending – with wooden steps to clamber up. Rather symbolic of his journey through life.

So, which is better? To wound them now? Farm them out early with the very best of intentions and a degree of involvement as 'the Process' takes control – ensuring a safe future and that a part of them will always feel unwanted? Or abandon them through death?

I begged him to reconsider, to try and keep his granddaughters with him. He obviously loved them to bits – a perverse remake of Brecht's Chalk Circle – prepared to let them go for an alleged better life. Proud, stubborn, loving, selfless, kind, decent Jack. His train pulled in as the tears started – his and mine – and he turned in the doorway – *"Don't say nothing"*.

"The train now approaching Platform 1 is on time, delayed, cancelled, blue or green, short or long – when it approaches – it is up to you to decide whether or not you choose to ride it. Remember to be grateful that you have a choice."

'Got any energy drinks?'
'Coffee.'

"The train now approaching Platform 1 is the 09.32 Southeastern service (blue train) to London Charing Cross calling at West St Leonards,

Crowhurst, Battle, Robertsbridge, Etchingham, Stonegate, Wadhurst, and Frant ..."

Frant was famous for smuggling during the 17th and 18th centuries and a turnpike road (now the A267) used to pass through there. The Rape of Pevensey and the Hundred of Rotherfield saw the village fall. Probably something to do with the Vikings.

Levy My Latte

THE COFFEE SHOP had been open for a while before a new war on waste, caused by disposable coffee cups, made headline news. Rightly so. However, I sit both sides of the fence. I love the planet, I love Sir David. I love the environment and support recycling. I am a small fish in a very big pond. I accept the cups I sell will invariably play their own part in the build-up of waste – along with every other piece of packaging for every single product on the planet.

Recycling – the new buzz word of the suddenly controversial coffee shop culture – overtaking 'alternative' milk. Recycling at a coffee shop that is only ever takeaway is quite practically impossible. The cups leave me, heading for a train and they become your responsibility. Station waste, where the coffee shop waste goes, is all recycled. I haven't seen recycling bins on trains or station platforms. Where will you choose to recycle your cup? Will you take it home with you after use and do it there? Or will you ensure you find somewhere along the way?

I do not have the answer. Nor do I have the deep pockets of the major players in the industry. I am an independent – if you put the cost on me – I cannot absorb all of it – so I will pass some on to you – and you may or may not absorb it, depending on your own pocket. If you do, I survive and you get your excellent, reasonably priced coffee – the counselling never incurs a charge. If you do not – I go under. There in a nutshell is the fate of the independent, dangling precariously above the jaws of the big sharks.

The big sharks are now 'selling' their take away cups – claiming that this is in line with their environmental policy. Really? Nothing to do with a clever marketing strategy to increase profit margins then. Prove yourselves. Give away your own-branded re-usable cups for nothing and I will become a believer.

The debate has sparked a new controversy in my shop. The handing over the counter of the customer's own re-usable cup. Brilliant – cry the ignorant, problem solved. No – the problem has just divided and multiplied. Let me explain.

I know where everything in my coffee shop has come from. The suppliers are regulated. The cups come in sterile, ready to use. All is clean, all is trackable, all will satisfy Environmental Health. My side of the counter is very much accounted for. Your side of the counter is not. Here lies the problem. I am starting to see a very interesting, and quite frankly unwelcome, assortment of re-usable cups.

My cups are, 4, 8 and 12 oz. Yours are usually much bigger – and you would like me to fill them up for you with hot, foaming, often alternative, milk – free of charge. The odd one would not make a difference. Several would – as the milk disappears out of the fridge and off the bottom line. Potentially this loss is offset by not using a paper cup. This is just one problem – these mixed sizes do not necessarily fit under the heads of my machine. I use a china shot cup to decant – to avoid un-necessary use of a paper one – my concession to the planet, provided you allow me to use the dishwasher to sterilise.

The bigger problem – with the greatest of respect – I do not know where your hands have been or where your cup has been. It may horrify you to know the number of customers who demand I make them a drink in their dirty re-usable cup with drink residue in the bottom, on the side, and on the rim. Some demand I wash their cup out first – and then have the cheek to come across all affronted when I tell them no – returning another day to complain about me to Tatz – who will only listen to so much before family loyalty kicks in. Oh – and if you hand me a dirty paper cup branded with the logo of another coffee shop and genuinely expect me to make you a drink in it – you have crossed a line. Would you take a dirty plate to a restaurant and ask them to serve your food on it? No – of course not – so why do you do exactly this to me? I cannot accept responsibility for the bacterial provenance of your reusable cup and risk contaminating my equipment, and possibly every subsequent customer – one of which might be The Ice Queen!

It took a global pandemic to simplify the policy – no re-usable cups ever again – it's safer for everyone this way – it always has been. We should continue to focus instead on the environment – it is everybody's responsibility.

Dramarama

IT IS AWKWARD when a stranger stands in front of the counter with tears streaming down their face. The fact that they feel comfortable enough to do so should probably be taken as a compliment. I hand out tissues and sympathy. Few are tears of joy – only mine when their train arrives – oh – and those of a young, local primary school care-taker when his phone pinged with a job offer as a holiday rep in Ibiza while he ordered his latte. He melted my heart when he went back to work, in his own time, for several weeks to check on the school ducklings in a cold snap.

On reflection, I have spent much of my life talking to people about their problems – possibly a missed calling. I don't mind. Everybody likes to feel needed – myself included. I only get frustrated when I think people have wasted my time. I have no patience for those who repeat the problem ad infinitum and then go on to repeat the behaviour that gave them the problem ad infinitum. Self-inflicted drama – find a backbone and make a change. I cannot make time, and do not have the inclination, to accommodate those who feed off my energy, requiring constant reassurance or propping up – day after day – until one day they see the light, solve their problem and disappear – never to be seen again – until the next time they have a problem. If you only have time for me when you are in a bad place – fuck off.

'Why is nobody in the ticket office? Right, then can I buy my ticket from you 'cos this is part of the station, isn't it?'
'No, sorry, this is the coffee shop.'
'Bloody hell. Well I *would* have had a coffee but I haven't got time now have I, because I don't know how to work the machine and you won't sell me a ticket.'

"The train now approaching Platform 1 is the 09.50 Southeastern service (blue train) to London Charing Cross calling at West St Leonards, Crowhurst, Battle, Robertsbridge, Etchingham, Stonegate, and Wadhurst …"

Wadhurst – originally Wadehurst – is an Anglo-Saxon Village probably deriving its name from Wada – a Saxon tribe, occupying the area in the 9th century, who began clearing the forests. Its smugness of today is not commensurate with its history.

The Coca-Cola Ad – St Leonards Style

REMEMBER THAT DIET Coke ad? The one involving a chiselled torso belonging to a shirtless construction worker taking a break – to the delight of some female office workers – all set to an Etta James sound track. The official line from Coca-Cola being 'it's not about the Diet Coke man being an object, it's not a voyeur thing, it's about cultural change, women being equal to men …' Oh please – it so was a voyeur thing for which we say thank you. Here is St Leonards version.

It was a long hot day in June, around 12.00 pm, (the lull, if you remember), and in he strolled. Shirtless, no definition, bit flabby, bit tattooed – he did love himself – which is fortunate as somebody had to. He sat down on the pew with his female accomplice. I knew I would spray it down with anti-bac as soon as they left. Trouble was brewing – I did not need it – it was 32 degrees inside the coffee shop. Mercury rising means tempers are at greater risk of fraying – not the best time to give luck a hefty shove.

I attempted to deflect the situation before it occurred, pointedly telling him it was warmer inside than out. He insisted he was fine inside on my pew, my personal pew. Unless you look like the Diet Coke Man – as in washed being the most minimum of requirements and are wearing some deodorant and a top – please get up and get out. He was waiting for his window of opportunity – which arrived with the entrance of another customer. Swiping a bottle of coke from the chiller, he swaggered out.

I resisted the temptation to unleash – remaining on the high ground. I followed him out and casually stood in my doorway watching the bastard. I am sure I could hear him gulping! There he stood on the platform – chugging from the bottle – looking me straight in the eye. Was I going to have a war over it? I really wanted to – the principle was calling me.

I weighed up the situation. If I had gone to war on a crowded platform, I would have given him the satisfaction of not only a successful theft, but also the opportunity for a BAFTA-worthy performance of injured innocence – which I am sure he has well-rehearsed and keeps up his sleeve – should he ever wear any (though perhaps he does, for special occasions like prison). It is not cool to lose it in public.

No – low life. No. Losing my cool was not going to happen. He is what he is because of his actions, and his life will always pan out the way it does for that same reason. Time will re-balance this small injustice with a justice. I needed to do nothing – comfortable in the knowledge that he will do it all for himself. Instead of making a scene, I gave him a cheery wave and returned behind the counter.

One for you one for me I pay for mine yours is free. One for you one for me. None for you.

"This is a security announcement. For your comfort and safety, closed circuit television is in use at this station."

'Hi Steve – usual?'
'Been keeping out of trouble?'
'Always – had the odd shoplifter recently.'
'Would you like some crime prevention advice?'
'Always'
'Clear everything off the counter.'
'Hilarious.'

Not My Circus, Not My Monkeys

A FAVOURITE SAYING of Seb's. He calmly repeated it to me as I tried in vain to dispatch him to rescue his sister from a teenage emotional drama. I was stuck at work unable to rescue her myself. He can be stubborn – not sure where he gets that from. The drama blew over as they typically do. Although deeply irritated at the time, I have found it is a statement with far reaching potential and one I have grown to love. It is most worthy of a place in any training manual.

'Not my circus, not my monkeys' is an old Polish idiom which means 'not my problem'. The intelligent application of the phrase requires a lightning-quick thought process followed by a swiftly executed processing strategy as follows:

Am I responsible for this situation? If so, it is my call to action and I had better get busy.

I am not responsible for this situation. I can now legitimately step back, guilt free, and watch the show unfold in front of me.

Learning which circus you belong to can be a useful tool for reducing impact and avoiding unnecessary stress in the workplace. The requirement for lengthy analysis and debate does not apply here. If you find yourself in a circus monkey situation and you feel the need to deliberate – go ahead – you will more than likely get swept up in a circus you could have avoided.

To put this analysis into practice behind the coffee shop counter:
'Not my circus' is the code – are you the ringmaster? No.
Is there a show going on the other side of the counter? Yes.
Please remain in your seat and watch the show. Your input will have no bearing on the outcome anyway.

Though it might be tempting, it is prudent *not* to establish exactly who the monkeys are or why they are performing – because any intervention will implicate you and it might well then become your circus. Yes – that is the voice of experience.

'Do you do skimmed milk?'
'Semi only.'
'In that case a large full-fat latte and a hot chocolate to take out please.'

Was the milk question relevant then if it did not matter? Or would you not have had a drink at all, if I had only done skimmed milk? Some questions have no answers.

Roberto and The Bowel Movement

ROBERTO'S ENCOUNTER WITH a fairly tricky, senior, female customer was priceless. It happened during the early shift – when there is no time to dither. Unable to decide on any particular coffee, she instead asked our least favourite question, particularly during rush hour, 'Do you have a toilet?'

Roberto explained we did not, aware that this particular sale was starting to become labour intensive and things were, shall we say, starting to back up. He tried again to ascertain what beverage she would like. She glared at him. *"What I really want is a Nescafe and a bowel movement."*

Roberto did not flinch. *"Well – we don't sell instant coffee and we do not have a toilet – so now you know for the future that those are two things you need to take care of before you leave the house!"*

'Could I have a decaf latte with soya milk and a pain-au raisin, no an oatmeal and raisin cookie, no an almond croissant – no a pain au raisin ...'
The train now approaching Platform 1... appears to have left without you.

"The train now approaching Platform 1 is the 10.45 Southern service (green train) to Brighton calling at Bexhill, Collington, Cooden Beach, Normans Bay, Pevensey and Westham, Eastbourne, Polgeate, Berwick, Glynde, Lewes, Falmer and Brighton ... "

Brighton, otherwise known as 'The Queen of Watering Places' (Poet Horace Smith), 'Old Ocean's Bauble', 'Doctor Brighton' and 'London by Sea.' The home of Pride – famous for its liberal perspective on life. Long may it last.

The Hurt Lockers

SERVING PEOPLE WITH a disability can be awkward. You want to be extra helpful – but extra help can have the reverse effect and be deemed patronizing and rude. You have to learn how to hold back while remaining on hand should help be needed.

I had an embarrassing incident with a man in sunglasses. I should be forgiven. I do have lots of customers who wear sunglasses inside because it looks cool, they have a hangover or they have been crying. I had seen this particular gentleman come in. He ordered a latte and then asked me to put the sugar in for him. I can't do this for everyone because the queue will back up. Instead, I pointed to the sugar shelf, brightly explaining that all the sugar is over there. He did not move – he just raised his stick in one hand and his guide dog took a step back. Fabulous – as I knew I would then have to feel bad about myself all day. He now comes in once a week, so clearly no hard feelings. I always put the sugar in the cup before making his latte – queue or no queue – he doesn't need to ask – we reached an understanding the first time.

Another customer doesn't need my help at all – he gets his coffee like anyone else and walks rather stiffly to the train. So, I had no idea. No idea that is until I was watching the News one evening and he featured on it. I had no idea that he had no legs. No idea that he stepped on a land mine in Afghanistan. I had no idea that his commitment to his photographic project on the Legacy of War could be so inspirational and heartbreakingly moving.

"Can we even say that war is over if people are still dying and lives are still disrupted decades after peace treaties are signed?"

Can we? The photographs – freeze framed individual hurt lockers of war. Look at the photographs and determine for yourself.

The next customer bustled in complaining about her day and how busy she was – trivial in comparison – I let her rattle on – my ears went deaf. I had just had an encounter with the very essence of humanity. I needed my head to digest it fully. Those that complain the least will often have justification to complain the most – the power and the volume of silence.

"The train now approaching Platform 1 is the 10.34 Southeastern service (blue train) to London Charing Cross calling at West St Leonards, Crowhurst, Battle, Robertsbridge, Etchingham, and Stonegate …"

Stonegate is an East Sussex village located at the cross of two old Roman roads – one linked Pevensey with the inland hills and the other linked Bardown (an old Roman ironworks) with the sea. Once the Romans had left, the area returned to its rural existence. I am sure the excitement they brought with them is missed.

Chapter 11

Matri-moany

'Usual please.'

'How are you?'

'It's my cousin's wedding this weekend – Biggin Hill – replacement buses – got to go into London and come back out again. Really distant cousin too, barely know him.'

'That's a bit of a bugger then.'

'Pardon? – Oh! I thought you said I wouldn't bother.'

'I wouldn't.'

I genuinely wouldn't. I am not a fan of weddings – I barely attended my own. I never dreamt of my wedding day – never thought about gowns, husbands, cakes (well not wedding cakes anyway), big receptions, flowers, or romantic locations. None of which are my idea of a perfect day. I avoid weddings like the plague – they feel so false – perhaps because divorce rates remain high – all that money – lavished on one day to prove to the world that two are now one – until divorce do us part. I also don't like being the centre of attention or being photographed. Maybe it's the commitment part that's the plague. I don't need to 'belong' to someone because I already belong to myself.

The problem could lie in the fact that I see marriage as 'is this it?' rather than 'this is it'. I find the whole concept of 'The Big Day' redundant. I appreciate it was necessary back in the days when a girl left home with her dowry and virginity – for a new love of her own – a copy of Mrs Beaton's Book of Household Management. That's a ripping read – which begs the question was the opportunity to legally have sex actually worth it.

I got married in a registry office one Friday morning with 7 guests and no cake, in a dress I had worn previously for riverside shenanigans. Just reading that statement back I realise my marriage was doomed from the start – because I entered in to it with no respect for the commitment – which is the same way I left it. My ex-husband cried when he made his vows (maybe he knew me better than I thought) – this just made me laugh – get a bloody grip man. Even when I said I do, I knew deep down I didn't – so did my China travelling companion – who refused to come and watch me make the biggest mistake of my life – I caught up with her on the flip side – she lived near Heathrow.

"In the interests of safety; the riding of skateboards, rollerblades and cycles on this Station is – still prohibited."

JJ

He most definitely was not my type. He was really – I just decided to pretend he was not. He decided to show me otherwise – his timing was good – I was over Station Man – time to move on – or at least flirt a little – and I do love a bad boy – their deviance is exciting.

He strode in through the coffee shop door and called me Treacle. Risky to call me Treacle. He politely asked for two teas with a discount, which he felt he deserved because he was doing some work for the next few days on one of the empty rooms further down the platform. I gave him the discount. I think it was his eyes, or maybe his voice, or because brazenness amuses me. I looked at the trail of building dust left everywhere as his calling card – thank you – thank you so very much. Discounted tea and a major clean-up operation. Little did I know the extent of the clean-up operation that would eventually be required.

JJ had a rough charm all of his own. He was spending quite a lot of money over the counter. Each time the twinkle in his eye sparkled a little more. His banter became less builder, more philosophical – oh and the building dust – there seemed to be no end to it. I think it was plaster dust – do not add water – it just compounds the problem – as I discovered.

He was well-travelled, fascinating, skilled and damaged. An ex-army diver now wearing an orange vest, armed these days with a bucket and trowel. Never judge a person by the job that they do – it is always an inaccurate form of measurement. He also knew what time I was leaving, and had pre-booked and pre-paid for a large tea to coincide with my departure – not his own. He had the balls to ask for his tea to be hand delivered (tea bag out). I agreed because delivering the tea would save more clearing up of builder's dust. I carried it to him – we stood talking for a while. Stig wandered down with his litter-picker in hand – just checking I was OK.

JJ was easy to talk to – so much to say – so much life experience. We had both lived overseas for many years. Travel is such a great leveller. We traded memories. He told me about his farm – a flashback for me to yet another life, another Scottish accent, Limousin cattle, country show grounds and the annual haul to the Perth cattle market – another love used up.

At the end of his second day he came in again. *"If I ask you very very nicely, will you give me your number?"*

"If you come back tomorrow and depending on how nicely you ask me, I will think about it." The confidence that a rib-cage height counter can give a woman. Being tall – he looked me straight in the eye – nodded, turned on his heel and left me a trail of dust as a parting gift. I helped myself to a coffee – the flirting was fun – but I knew I would never see JJ again.

Never – until he strode back in the next day around lunchtime, informed me that he was there to ask me incredibly nicely for my number. I contemplated giving him a false number – *"don't even think about it as I am going to punch it straight into my phone"* – he waited for mine to ring. Connection made – the game was on. I loved the 'po-ta-to, po-ta-to' thump of his Harley Davidson – it invited me to feel new freedom. Some of my happiest moments have been spent flying through mountains and whipping round twisting passes on the back of a motorbike – my senses heightened – my thoughts unharnessed.

We did drinks, chemistry, dinners, antique shops, history and beaches – all sounding too perfect? Of course it was. He told me we were embarking on a journey of a lifetime and he swore he would be the one that was there at the end. At the end of what? JJ didn't add up – and bad boys typically come bad. It took me some time to figure out that not all of his gear was for diving. Zero tolerance – no exceptions. Goodbye JJ – I can't deal with your shit – I appreciate the apology – I am moving on. I have to admit to a small grin when he phones me periodically out of the blue claiming he misses me. He doesn't – it is the audacity of the call that makes me smile – reminding me why I liked him in the first place. I never go backwards – when something is over – its best left. Ian is not an exception – because in my mind he was a continuance. My eyes are firmly forward.

"The train embarking on a journey of a life time has been delayed."
"This is due to a signalling failure."
"Mind the gap – the gap between truth and reality."

Reverse Bastardization

A COLD, HARD truth needs facing. Maybe this was the time. Men – attracting them is one thing – staying with them is something entirely different. Station Man, JJ, Psychopath, Ex-Husband – I could analyse all the way back to the 1980s. It's not you it's me? I'm usually much quicker to spot a trend.

I have to admit to myself that I may be subconsciously troubled. I know the war lies within. A private battle stemming from the rejection that inevitably follows adoption and the subsequent death of a parent. This fear makes me defensive. Bollocks – I have no hope of finding perfection after all. I wanted to be perfect to prove I am lovable. However, I might stand a better chance of being happy with someone other than myself, if I accept what is and look to exhaust the trend.

If abandonment is what I am really frightened of, then I must crave love in the form of a stable relationship, based on a trust I can rely on. To achieve this – I have to stop inadvertently (fucking it up) sabotaging the possibility of a relationship becoming intimate. Striving for perfectionism to extinguish a fear of intimacy tends to push the right people away. Whatever a right person is matters not because I refuse to be a victim. Where are those plasters? I think I will go for a long fast drive on a road to nowhere with something heavy on maximum volume.

Wiccapedia

SOMEWHERE AMONG THE grand buildings and the hustle and bustle of gentrification, hides another strand of St Leonards DNA – fancy dress and a touch of all things Wicca. The town can't get enough of contemporary paganism – it is a Sussex phenomenon.

The darker side are keen to promote a recalcitrant persona – opting for head to foot in black – looking more Manson than Masonic. They embrace witchcraft, devil worship and the occult. I do not find them unnerving because here in St Leonards, everyone tries so hard to stand out, that they all fit in. Eccentricity can go full circle.

The lighter side of a Pagan is often a simple pentacle around the neck. I opt for a Tiffany heart, very un-St Leonards I know, but as we are discussing branding it seems relevant, but I do find the Pentacle symbol quite appealing – the star representing the elements of earth, wind, fire and water plus spirit (rather like the gold spandex band from the 80's), encircled to symbolise their reciprocal relationship. Not dissimilar to the elements required to make a good latte. I keep an open mind.

'Great costume – what is the occasion?'
'Going to our best friend's funeral.'
'I'm so sorry.'
'Don't be – we can hear him laughing up above.'

If you see eccentric attire in February then its Fat Tuesday, if its May Day weekend then it's time for Jack in the Green – the local pagan festival recognising the divinity of nature. Jack is the symbol of winter – when he is killed – summer can begin. Leaves and branches are given to the crowd to keep until the winter solstice in late December – they then burn them to rid any bad spirits. Perhaps we should keep some under the counter in case any harpies come in.

There is always something going on and the coffee shop is happy to provide a leaflet shelf – a popular resource and a great way of finding out what is going on in the local community. More importantly – these individual flyers are tangible markers of the ebb and flow created by ever-changing social relationships on which communities are built and society is based. Fluidity allows for growth.

I am always happy to accept leaflets from local people if it helps promote their own business, the Arts or a good cause – diverse mouthpieces shouting out over the seagulls. It is my acknowledgment of encompassment, of reciprocity, of difference, of co-operation and occasionally they conflict. They sit brightly coloured and informative next to the sugars above the bin, turning into confetti on a windy day, as they blow around the shop driving us crazy. These passionate leaflets show the very heart of the community – dog groomers, dog walkers, cinema, festivals, recruitment agencies, bloggers, schools, jewellery makers, wallpaper workshops, hospice lotteries, yoga, tarot, hairdressers, weight watchers, landscape gardeners, and roofers. I feel strangely proud to form part of it.

Culture and society are intrinsically linked. Society consists of the people who share a common culture, whereas a culture consists of the objects of society. Culture is a way that groups of people and individuals define themselves. People can share a common culture from a mutual geographic location. These are the layers of society. I like to consider myself cultured.

"The train now approaching Platform 1 is the 10.53 Southeastern service (blue train) to London Charing Cross calling at West St Leonards, Crowhurst, Battle, Robertsbridge, and Etchingham ..."

Etchingham was a manor owned by the de Achyngham family. The 'Etchingham' family records indicate that William was so pleased with his right-hand man that he gave him the land now known as Etchingham. It is prone to flooding and gossip.

Church of the Poisoned Mind

THE LEAFLET SHELF is my favour to the local community. I believe in free speech and am not here to censor what does or does not go on the shelf. There is no charge for displaying the leaflets. I am simply happy to have them.

I certainly did not appreciate the attitude of this particular occasional customer. Sometimes a customer can call in and I am there alone. Other times there is a crowd – all leaping on the same train. This woman picked a crowded moment to voice her complaint – loudly. Shock horror – I found myself face to face with a 'Venting Complainer'.

Grabbing a leaflet from the shelf in one hand and dragging her soap box in the other – she proceeded to stand on it in the middle of the coffee shop and give me and everyone else a lecture about this particular leaflet. I think a bollocking is a better word. My face was neutral – my eyes were not.

The offending article was a promotional flyer inviting us all to 'relax, release and receive'. The producer of said leaflet claimed to be 'an urban medicine woman' whose work 'assists people to uncover the innate wisdom, beauty and strength that lies within us.' She specialises in Access Bars (points on the head – not the alcoholic variety) and uses metamorphic technique on reflex points.

According to the uninvited lecturer, this leaflet was not promoting these things. Instead, it was a cover up for a new wave of the Scientology movement which was infiltrating the country. If you are unaware of what Scientology is – here is a brief overview. Scientology does not preach or impose a particular idea of God on Scientologists. It allows personal awareness to develop and as it does so, people are expected to discover the truth through their own observations. This path of discovery leads them on to become fully fledged Scientologists.

Apparently, having this leaflet on the shelf made me socially and morally irresponsible. Much was apparent to this excitable speaker, though not her flagrant trespass of an unwritten rule of the coffee shop, which prohibits anyone coming in and dictating to me what I will and will not do – unless its station staff in an emergency obviously.

I am very capable of defending myself. To make this clearer to her, I walked around the counter, picked up the leaflets in question and moved them to a more prominent position. I then turned to the Spouter and told her my customers have a choice – albeit more extensive than that of Hobson – but the sentiment is the same – take it or leave it – pick up a leaflet – or not. They are perfectly capable of making up their own minds. I also, out of the kindness of my heart, enlightened her with the thought that if someone is stupid enough to turn some kind of alternative beauty therapy session into an attempt at religious radicalisation, then there really is little hope for them.

Relax and Release. Breathe and Receive.
Relax and Release – and there's her train.

While I am on the subject of the shelf – it gets used for all sorts of things. Some people store their laundry powder on it while they wait for a train – or scribble some notes or read every leaflet backwards and put them back on the wrong piles. Just say you want to stand in and wait for a train – you don't have to buy anything – it just lessens the load for both of us – you do not have to pretend to be incredibly interested in something you are not and I do not have to tidy up after you.

'Strong coffee – extra shot today.'
'I know the feeling.'

Put on a Show

"WHAT CAN I get you?"

I had to wait for them to stop kissing before they would answer me – displays of public affection do not offend me – it's the slurping noise that revolts me.

As I made lattes for the couple, I could not help but notice the love bites on their necks – badges of dominance blended in amongst the tattoos – inkings of their own defiance.

Slurping aside, I am not a fan of the tattoo – Tatz is aware of this and I was 'disappointed' when she broke rank. I referred her to the Company policy on tattoos and piercings. There isn't one really – I just don't like them – particularly on women – I know – how very sexist of me. Each to their own – I shall not be getting 'inked'. Perhaps it's the permanence of the commitment I struggle with.

Catch Me if You Can

This game was invented by the timetable creators. Green trains rumble in on the 'other side' from the Eastbourne direction. Green trains rumble out from 'our side' for the Eastbourne direction – but we also have blue train thunder – heading out on a different track route for Tunbridge Wells and beyond. The arrival of a green train does not coincide with the departure of the blue train – and probably not even with another green train.

Sometimes I hear shouting from the platform and know that it comes from yet another unwitting player who has lost this frustrating game. The timetabling arrangements at St Leonards are not sophisticated enough to incorporate a 'connection' facility, so this means that if you arrive on the opposite, incoming platform, you have may have 90 seconds to sprint over the footbridge – praying that Stig has spotted any dog mess before your foot does – run out onto the station concourse then hairpin turn straight back in through the booking hall – minding out for the slippery when wet tiles on a rainy day – in order to leap red-faced on to the outward-bound train.

The green train is not connected to the blue train – the blue train is not connected to the green train – this is important information because if you are arriving on the green train and you can actually see the blue train coming in – taking into account the footbridge factor and the line of passengers in the booking office – you are almost guaranteed to miss the wing and a prayer to Charing Cross by a frustrating 3 seconds. But at least the coffee shop is there, and you can have a sit down on the pew to recover.

'Sorry no toilets at the Station.'
'Oh no. Where is the nearest one?'
'Across the square if you buy something, down by the Pier if you don't.'

'How far is that?'
'You won't make it.'

Give Me A Break

I AM ALWAYS envious of customers who come in sparkling from head to foot with invigoration that can only be got from swimming in the sea. I have many customers with split second timing. Circus Silks is one of them. We always just make it – sometimes the lid doesn't – because it takes two seconds to snap one on. As an aerial silk performer, split second timing is her trademark. She invited me to one of her classes – sensing a trip to the fracture clinic – I politely declined.

Circus Silks walked in one day, beautifully re-charged, glowing with Greek sunshine, and told me in no uncertain terms that I should take a break. Sound advice. I knew I was tired. She was right. I mulled it over for a month or so and then, on the spur of the moment, I dropped my own silk.

"The train now approaching Platform 1 is the Southern service (green train) … To Gatwick …"

Everybody needs a holiday sometimes – far flung or gently stretched – it doesn't matter which. What does matter is taking the time to step back, reflect and re-charge. But when you have your own business, just the thought of having a holiday is exhausting. I have to trust someone to take over the helm. I plan, foresee, write lists, think about every eventuality just for the business – I then have to decide who wants to come on holiday. Teenagers are tricky creatures – they do not tend to put holiday and parent in the same category. Participants established, I then plan the holiday for all those coming, and for anyone abstaining. I then have to plan, foresee, write lists and think about every eventuality for those left behind. Fortunately, I have people I can rely on who can help me make it all possible.

Self-indulgently, I booked somewhere far away – no teenagers – no business – no responsibility – no time constraints. As I relaxed into the seat of long haul, I congratulated myself on being brave enough to leave my work mobile behind. It was me that needed re-charging.

Barrister Thursday

'What a dreadful day – by god I am not missing this train.'

Coat matched suit matched shirt matched tie matched briefcase matched glasses – terribly posh and very sharp. It must be Barrister Thursday, the favoured service being the 12.34 to London Charing Cross.

Professing himself in need of a panini and a strong coffee, he took a moment to explain to me. It was a Family Law matter and he held his own court in front of my counter, where I became the defendant, the witness and the judge. A theatrical five minutes and an education. Shared custody – explain and discuss – so we did.

For those fortunate enough not to know about these things, shared custody is becoming more prevalent in England. In many circumstances, this is a positive step because the best interests of the child are paramount, and the law considers that a child has an entitlement to a mother and a father. However – and this was part of his headache – it can be futile to continue to labour the point to one's client that shared custody is unlikely to be granted to the parent that repeatedly punched the other parent in the face. Cue eye roll, raised hands in an 'I rest my case,' theatrical gesture of resignation, and fourteen long strides out of the door onto the 12.34.

I stopped for a moment to contemplate how different my life might have been if I had invested all my energy into studying rather than hell raising. I think I would have made a good barrister – certainly a formidable interrogator. My life would have been different – of course it would have – but not necessarily better – because my life has been colourful – not just black and navy. I also do not believe in regretting choices – I accept some are better than others – but we learn far more when we fuck up. I am proud to be so knowledgeable.

Twelve Good Men

Jury Service. Two dreaded words spoken over the counter. I have never been called in this country for jury service. I would enjoy listening to a good trial and the mental flex of deductive reasoning. Not everyone shares my view.

A jury is usually a body of 12 people, (men and women since the 1920s), sworn in to give a verdict based on the evidence submitted to them in a court of law. We, as people, on the whole seem very happy to pass judgment on anything and everything without ever having listened to any supporting evidence. Why is it then that when faced with the opportunity to pass judgment with evidence, the very same people suddenly lose their nerve and decide that being judgemental is not for them after all?

St Leonards must have been on some alphabetical system for calling jurors, as we went through several months with new jurors coming through every week. Nobody discussed the cases – I got an occasional shaky outline.

What most jurors passing through the coffee shop found frustrating was the unknown time element of being part of the service. It could be a couple of days or a couple of weeks. Financial implications also had an impact. One elderly couple came every day – completely unfamiliar with public transport, terrified of timetables, trains, courts and anything generally out of their comfort zone. The wife came to see the husband onto the train for moral support. They were struggling to make ends meet. You can reclaim travel and sustenance costs incurred when on jury service – but this was not paid in advance and they were scrabbling for the train fare. For them jury service seemed to cause private hardship – albeit temporary.

One woman was desperate to get inside the court and pass judgement. Waiting to be called is a bit like being a sub for a sports team – a certain number of players have to be available to enable the court hearing to happen but not everyone gets selected. I think, not that I am making a judgment obviously, that it may have been in the defendant's favour, because she was part-woman, part-Rottweiler – and you should at least try to keep an open mind until the summing up of all evidence. The whole point is that you assess, analyse and weigh everything up, not devour the facts in one huge bite, only to find you regurgitate a snap decision.

Everybody else I talked to on their way to court was absolutely dreading the experience. The leopard-skin juror was a riot. Multiple animal prints were her view of smart, and I would not swear on a bible, (I wouldn't anyway), that she had not had a cheeky sherbet on the way down to the station. She ordered a strong coffee as I couldn't run to a gin and tonic, swore an awful lot and said she was not looking forward to the day.

I asked her what she was afraid of. She said she did not want to be recognised by anybody on trial, because if you convict someone, they have families and those families will come to get you. That is a legitimate fear, because in the minds of some, justice does not necessarily stop at the court room door. She had no faith in the criminal justice system, nor anything remotely Establishment, or that the spiked heel of her left shoe would remain attached to the sole and ensure her safe arrival in the court room. I watched her teeter towards the train. Did she make it? The jury remains out.

'Salt & vinegar crisps twice love.'
'How are you?'
'Moved here permanently now, so I won't see you so much love.'
No more boring the pants off me then. Hoorah.

"The train now approaching Platform 1 is the 10.53 Southeastern service (blue train) to London Charing Cross calling at West St Leonards, Crowhurst, Battle and Robertsbridge ..."

Robertsbridge dates back to 1176. Abbot Robert de St Martin founded a Cistercian abbey there. A Bruderhof community resides in underskirts on its outskirts.

Chapter 12

Discount from the Boss

'Two teas and a diet coke.'
'Boss said they are on the house.'

Every now and then there is a crackdown of some kind at the Station. Sometimes it is Revenues from the Train Company looking for fare dodgers – or those passengers who wanted to purchase a ticket but were unable to do so because the ticket office is closed – if you are feeling more benevolent about the crime. Fare dodgers are a drain on railway profits which in turn help keep ticket prices up. I believe the guards on the train, if you can find one not striking, are incentivised with every sale – be warned.

The first time I witnessed a Revenue crack down at St Leonards I genuinely thought there had been a terrorism threat or attack of some kind. Uniforms were everywhere, barricading the exits both sides of the platform. It felt quite intimidating – which I suppose is the point. Many people with a ticket missed their train because they could not get past the blockade in time. To be fair – the numbers issued with penalty notices were probably greater.

I understand that it is an offence to ride the train without a ticket. I understand that it defrauds or detracts money away from the railway and that all the money is needed so it can be reinvested into new trains, more staff and badly needed engineering work. I understand all that. What I do not understand is when you, Mr Revenue Inspector, then come into the coffee shop and attempt a pathetic blag at free loading off me.

"I was told I could have these drinks for free" – is how the conversation started.
"Oh really", I said, *"and who told you that?"*
"The Boss told me. He said all I had to do is come in here and ask you and I could have the drinks on the house – because we are working on the platform."
My face darkened. There are chancers – and then there are piss takers.
"I am the Boss!!!"

He left my revenue on the counter with his delusions of grandeur. Next time, do not come in when you are laying down the law to the world about the morality of free-loading off the railways, then try it on with me.

This particular month, the Council were issuing Fixed Penalty Notices at the front of the Station. These notices were for littering and environmental offences to the tune of £80. Judging by the feedback and the language heard in the coffee shop, I think it's fair to say these notices have not been well received.

'It was only a cigarette end.'
'You do know you cannot put a lit cigarette end in a full bin?'
'FFS. Have they got nothing better to do with their time? Jobsworth.'

Your view probably depends on whether you were caught, your

definition of littering, or whether you are Stig, the person who has to continually go around after the litterers, to sweep, retrieve and deposit it in the correct place. It depends if you think about the environment, public areas, and whether you have any kind of social conscience. Today the cigarette end – tomorrow the fly-tipped sofa with matching arm chair. This is not an exaggeration. There actually is a three-piece suite on the pavement just outside the station boundary. It doesn't really add to the ambience of the area, but is useful if you are still waiting for a replacement bus.

Less littering would, in real terms, mean less time spent by the station staff cleaning up after the general public and more time with the window blind up. What would you prefer?

Oh – and a shout out to the repeat offender who lets their dog foul on the station cross bridge and leaves it there for the station staff to clean up so everybody else doesn't accidentally walk in it. Definitely FPN worthy, but the dog offends when there is no one around to hold them accountable. I personally feel dog mess is a far greater offence than a cigarette end – but FPNs do not appear to have categories on a sliding scale. I think they should introduce them.

'You won't believe what just happened.'
'Try me.'
'I just got a ticket for littering'
'Thank god it wasn't for shitting – trust me – this happens too often.'

Swinging with Unicorns

THERE WAS, HOWEVER, one customer who I genuinely felt sorry for – because he is a decent human being and how he spends his spare time is none of my business. He absent-mindedly stubbed his cigarette out on the pavement outside the station before coming in for a hot chocolate. Always on his way to various meetings. Always exhausted. He works in the construction sector for care homes – specialising in design, budget and funding.

He campaigns for better facilities for people suffering with chronic kidney disease. He explained that kidney disease is as prevalent as cancer and heart disease but we hear relatively little about it. I fast-tracked his loyalty card for a free hot chocolate. He does worthwhile work for people in need, with a good attitude and a positive outlook.

He went on to explain budgeting constraints to me in layman's terms. If it was a relative of mine who had to go in to care, would I not expect the contractor to spend more on their room than the price of a 'Skinners Garden Shed'? Obviously, I would, but apparently this is not the case. I have reflected on that statement a lot recently – along with the eleventh commandment – Thou Shalt Not Litter. Really – thou shalt not.

What I did not know about him, and still wish I didn't, is that by night he is a bi-sexual party swinger who likes to indulge all fetishes adult with his open-minded Unicorn. Not the mythical variety – the other kind – the bisexual woman who agrees to be the third component in a threesome experience. Possibly equally rare, hence the name. In hindsight, this penchant is probably the reason for his exhaustion at a relatively young age. Hard nights partying, escorting, educating dressing, undressing, whipping, rubber, groups of both sexes diving suits, masks, chains, accessories, torture, restraint, vibration, gyration, fornication – too much information. I wonder if he knows Miami Vice? That's an aforementioned customer – not a request.

Despite being invited, I have avoided entering the inner sanctum of his social life via the photographs on his phone, by refusing to look. I have also had cause to raise my hand to stop him discussing sole distributor opportunities for vibrators – leaving the irony of the opportunity to reverberate around the coffee shop walls. Some things should really be left to the imagination. The coffee shop strictly observes the 9am watershed – thank you.

'Two coffees love – mind if we sit here?'
'You can if you tell me why you are wired?'
'Drug bust – incoming – next train.'

Strike A Pose

Philmore, of Portobello Road fame, also resides in St Leonards and has brought his own fashion label with him. Philmore designs and makes clothes tailored to the individual – and whilst I am not a lover of the word bespoke – because it has been flogged to death and is generally overrated – bespoke is what he does. I know St Leonards is very lucky to have him and I can highly recommend him.

Having come runner up to a gin company in the Sussex Business Awards for Best New Business with a Woman at the Helm, I needed an evening dress not made of denim for the awards ceremony. Gin versus coffee – now some may argue that is a very difficult decision – if you find it difficult first thing in the morning – there are groups that can help you.

At the time of nomination, I was of course flattered and patted myself on the back for good effort. I took a couple of friends and my key staff member at the time – Tatz – for a fairly expensive evening of glitz, glamour and a few more business lessons as follows.

In order to attend the Gala dinner and final award ceremony, you had to purchase tickets and preferably a table of 10. Even more preferable – you should also have attended the semi-final dinner – cocktails and dinner – (different dress) – again at a cost per ticket. Personally, I feel if you have won something or been nominated to receive an award, it is churlish to expect you to pay for the privilege. But that is sometimes how networking is – cash for contacts.

The sad part about my somewhat cynical view, is that despite there being some truly amazing women there, I felt disappointed that here we are in two thousand and something – and we still feel the need to have an award with a 'Woman at the Helm'. Why? We can congratulate ourselves for making strides towards a neutral-gender society – and for some it has been a walk in the park – but here we are supporting, paying for and enforcing an award just for women. We really are our own worst enemy.

My award certificate – the one I had to write in several times about as it was presented to me with the Company name spelt incorrectly, someone may have been on the gin, does not sit proudly on the coffee shop wall. Instead it is slung in a filing cabinet. An award making me a runner up of Best Start Up Business of the Year – irrelevant of whether a man, woman or monkey is at the helm – would have been worth receiving.

Because Philmore was local and had supported me with his custom, it was only polite to reciprocate. I asked him to make me a dress for the above occasion. My days of dressing up are in the wardrobe to Narnia – and these days Casual and me work together just fine.

Philmore picked up on my embarrassment and reluctance, and whilst he could not have made this any easier for me, I made it quite hard for him. I apologise. I am not a lover of the frock, nor do I spend hours in front of a mirror or taking selfies. Rather than force me to attend several fittings at his place of work, I opted for a budget remake of 'Mohammed and the Mountain' – he came to me and we had dress fitting lock-ins after hours in the coffee shop.

We had a good laugh as he measured, discreetly writing the measurements where I could not see them. He reappeared a few days later with the dress, which he re-fitted and pinned – a process which needed repeating. We were in the middle of the final fitting. The coffee shop door was locked. I had most of my clothes on – certainly the important ones – and my jeans – obviously – because I believe it is perfectly good practice to try on all sorts of clothes over those you already have on.

I was half in and half out of the dress and Philmore was helping it over my top half as it was covered in pins in awkward places. Suddenly, the coffee shop door burst open. I had not pushed the lock down correctly. In walked a parched customer. Her horrified expression made her mouth fall open.

"No. No", I said, *"it is not what you think. We are having a dress fitting."*
"Really?" said Parched sarcastically.
"Yes really!" We were.

In a grand gesture, she swept a bottle of water from the chiller, put her money on the counter, said she had absolutely no inclination to know what was really going on, and swept out. I collapsed in hysterical laughter – while Philmore, consummately professional, continued his work without dropping a pin.

"This is a safety announcement … please take extra care whilst on the station."

'Do you sell beer?'

'No sorry.'

'Got a bottle opener then?'

'Probably.'

'Thanks sweetheart – you're a darling.'

'You're welcome.'

Wired for Sound

I HAD A conversation with Philmore about the seemingly innocent potato crisp. There they are in the basket on the counter all tucked up in their cleverly branded, sealed duvet, calling you to buy them for the long train journey ahead. And you do, in great quantities. But Philmore and I have a love hate relationship with crisps. We both enjoy eating them – what's not to like – but they should carry a warning on the packaging – similar to that of a cigarette packet – crisps can seriously harm the mental health of those around you. If you do not understand then I cannot emphasise enough how lucky you are.

Time for some raising of public awareness. Misophonia is sound sensitivity – occurring when people are emotionally affected by sounds made by others. Certain sounds trigger emotional responses that some might consider unreasonable given the circumstances.

If I could wave a magic wand and change one thing about myself it would be this – the fact that I suffer from it is as irritating as the noises that drive me to distraction. It is equally irritating for those who do not suffer – as they do not understand why they are getting the death glare. There is no known cure. I find the consumption of crisps by others in a confined space disturbing, as do so many other people, even though they probably do not want to admit it so openly. For some, the negative impact to something like hearing crisp consumption, triggers a fight-or-flight response – tricky when confined to a carriage.

You have caught your train, you are in motion. Everybody is enjoying a nice peaceful ride on the train. Then the early warning sign that any calm is about to be destroyed. There it is, the distinctive crinkle of a bag, as a fellow passenger starts to wrestle it out of its hiding place. Eating crisps in confined public places can only be described as antisocial behaviour – worthy of a fine.

While I am on the subject, I find the throat noise of an excessive gulper intolerable. Likewise, popcorn in cinemas – madness. Apples – a definite no – only soft fruits should be consumed in public. We cannot sell apples, just in case somebody buys one and eats it on the pew – torturing me for the entirety of its consumption. Crunching or gulping anything in the coffee shop is also considered antisocial behaviour – forcing me to turn on the steam wands to mask the noises – and if that fails – I will put my hands over my ears – silently praying a queue does not start to form, as this will obviously require my immediate attention and the use of my hands.

Misophonia started when I was 11. I suddenly found family mealtimes intolerable – the sounds of chewing and swallowing of others were infuriating. I did not understand why – and neither did my family. My mother decided to find a solution to my problem – believing a pair of tractor ear defenders would do the trick. So, there I sat with defenders adorning my ears, not only cross, but looking stupid as well. There is new research to suggest that misophonia may be heavily connected to recalling bad experiences from the past – including wearing ear defenders at meal times! It also gets worse with age or the forming of intimate relationships. Excellent – only the age to concern myself with then.

Philmore has devised a clever coping strategy that works for him – he carries an emergency packet of crisps about his person. When he hears the crinkling of a crisp packet, followed by the inevitable eardrum shattering crunch, as each potato crisp is devoured in the same way a dog destroys a bone – when he hears those sounds – he reaches in his bag for his emergency supply and drowns out the noise with crunching of his own – thereby committing the same offence. Brilliant – but only for those of us who not only remembered to bring our own sound-combatting supply with us, but who also have the requisite self-control not to eat the snack prematurely, thereby losing their edible form of self-defence.

Should you need a supply, crisps can be found on the coffee shop counter – large basket at the back – right hand side – underneath the invisible sign that says 'must be consumed off the premises.' I expect sales to increase.

'Two teas to take away and two cookies love.'
'Do you think I can balance them on top of each other?'
'Not really – they are very hot.'
'Don't worry love – I used to be in the circus.'
'Well then – you are in the right place.'

Bohemian Rhapsody

'Can I help?'
'I think I've lost something.'

Passengers are surprisingly forgetful, but people at St Leonards are equally surprisingly good at handing in lost property – usually into the ticket office – but sometimes to me over the counter – mobile phones in particular. Useful to also know that Southeastern have a central property collection point at Cannon Street and a website form to reunite the lost with the found. I tested the system having dropped a cardigan in a rush to change trains – I have never seen the cardigan again.

Joan of Arc, part heroine and part martyr. Unconventional, determined and dignified. I know she supports the taking of difficult paths and is certainly not scared to stand up for what she believes in. She likes to crusade on a principle in a completely different way to me. She's an interesting combination of Dutch London with a bit of French Resistance – we have had several cappuccinos on the pew.

Joan is alternative and a bit ditzy – but that is a pre-requisite for a happy life at St Leonards. Having lived in the back of beyond, somewhere in very rural France – in a run-down dwelling with no basic supply of power and water – she was having a few adjustment issues living in a building that actually had both. The sort of existence that is classed as bohemian and character building and can only be endured by bohemians of character in the first place.

I am no stranger to a bohemian existence. I once saw an advert in The Henley Standard – houseboat on a private mooring for sale. I have always been an early riser – the ink on the newspaper was still drying – I phoned – I saw – I purchased. This is me doing commitment my way – diving straight in. A more prudent purchaser would have probably had the boat surveyed – or at least looked at it properly – before walking quickly in the opposite direction. I have always been good at seeing a bigger picture.

There she was. 'Ondine' – water nymph or female spirit. An old Dutch fishing barge complete with a Viking-esque bowsprit and sailing wings. The original mast had been removed and was lying up the side of the garden. Residential moorings on the Thames are incredibly hard to come by because so few exist. This mooring was an entire private garden and an old wooden garage – the Thames happened to be at the bottom of the garden. Ondine was nestled under a willow tree – delightful – what a romantic and tranquil place to live. Money changed hands quickly and I moved in during the spring time.

It was romantic to a degree – but certainly not luxurious. The toilet and shower were in the garage on dry land – the flooring was a bit rotten – I found it best to be quick when using the facilities – in case they fell through the boards. The kitchen was a bit of marble on top of a working Perkins V6 engine and to cook anything required a scramble on deck to turn the gas cylinder on. I am sure it leaked as it always smelt of gas – so I only turned it on when I really needed to. I wasn't eating often then anyway so it mattered very little. In case it rained heavily, the bilge pump switch was located next to the TV socket – I was all set. I got used to the swans pecking on the side of the boat in the middle of the night and the gentle swaying whenever I walked on dry land.

Winter was where the romance ended. Heavy storms meant the Thames burst its banks in the night – I woke up to find myself marooned. I immediately understood why the garage was on stilts and the need for an emergency walkway the length and height of the fence. The flooding was so bad that the fence was already under water. I phoned the Squadron Leader (Mother) who had a dinghy in her garage – as only someone worthy of the title would. She arrived on site, removed the dinghy from the car roof and rowed across my garden to rescue me – and off she went – home to dry land and dry socks. I stood there holding the painter – looking at my commitment rather differently. I persevered. I have never been so cold at night. I got chilblains and my duvet froze with condensation. The water rats moved in under the floorboards and dragged half my clothing below to make a nest. But at least the view was to die for.

I stayed because I am hard core, will rise to a challenge – or am plain stupid – take your pick. I came home from work one day and realised my socks were getting wet as I watched TV. I didn't panic until my ankles were wet. May Day May Day. The emergency services response time was excellent. I think they couldn't resist the call because I had 3 fire engines with crews and the river police there all at the same time. They were laughing their arses off – they had an emergency pump running on full – comments such as 'it would be quicker to pump out the Thames' and 'why don't you put the plug back in?' A night I will never forget – as slowly my pathetic assortment of possessions made their way on to the lawn. I lost all my photos and my vinyl record collection. One of the fireman picked up a butter knife (boating essential!) and showed me how it went straight in through every beam – just like the butter it was meant for. The boat was rotten and deemed a floating liability. Bollocks.

I am resourceful and managed to flog it to some Dutch Barge Enthusiast – aka – nutter – for £1 if he took it away. I still have that £1 – one of the most important deals of my life. If the boat had sunk I would have been liable for the cost of salvage – this would have run into thousands – as Henley-on-Thames is not known for its shipwrecks. The enthusiast filled the hole with cement – fired up the engine – reckless and brave as the boat was shaking violently – and whacked it in reverse – away he went – in reverse – which seemed to be the only direction the boat went in. I sat on the bank for quite some time watching them circling in reverse – round and round they went. Their problems just beginning – mine were over. I popped a cork.

I don't like to admit defeat as you know – so I designed and commissioned a replacement. I slept in the garage for 6 months until an empty shell arrived on a low loader. Rising to a new challenge, I fitted it out with the help of a local builder.

I understand bohemian – I understood Joan. Once a former teacher of delinquent children – she travelled the world – loved and lost – her glasses are often lost even though they are perched on top of her head. This makes me laugh – I do it all the time. I am in spectacle denial. I know I need them to read – wearing them on my head is the first step to acceptance.

Joan is passionate about her little car that gave her the freedom she craved to move about between the seaside and the hidden villages – she is also a roamer. One day she came in to the coffee shop distraught and frustrated. Her car had been stolen. She had been to the police and was outraged to receive a crime number followed by a Case Closed. She was determined to track it down – I did not hold out much hope for its safe return.

A week or so later she came back in. I asked her about her car and was abruptly shut down. Joan then relented. She was very embarrassed because her car had not actually been stolen. Instead she had forgotten where she had parked it and had a huge shock when she walked past and saw it sitting there – right where she had left it.

I gave her a cappuccino on the house, and somewhere amongst the foam and the chocolate, Joan found her sense of humour. We dissolved into hysterical laughter.

"The train now approaching Platform 1 is the 11.53 Southeastern service (blue train) to London Charing Cross calling at West St Leonards, Crowhurst, and Battle ..."

Battle is a small town in East Sussex – 55 miles south of London. Famous as the site of the 1066 Battle of Hastings. Here William, Duke of Normandy, defeated King Harold II to become William 1 in 1066. It lies within a designated area of outstanding beauty somewhere near the Potting Shed.

Chapter 13

Tribalism

ALONE ON THE pew at the end of the day – reflecting on the trials and tribulations – I realised that Joan had let me in … and that she was not my only customer to do so. It was no longer a 'them and me' situation because, imperceptibly over time and over the counter, I had created a niche for myself, as well as my business. These were real relationships. I locked up and walked down the platform, feeling a strange and unfamiliar sense of belonging which I found somewhat unsettling.

Railway Children – Commuters in Training

'What would you like?'
'Regular Flat White please.'
'Beautiful day – but that wind.'

'Hi could I have a soya latte – what do you want darling? A hot chocolate? Yes? You would like a hot chocolate? No? What then precious? No, you are not having coke – you can have hot chocolate or water or a babyccino …'

As you would expect, our child customer base increases during school holidays. This is a mixed blessing as groups of indecisiveness slow down the queue. Sometimes queue jumping has to be permitted – I am sure even Lady Antebellum would concede on rare occasions. There are already a few young regulars who come in during term time for a bad breakfast choice – even though we do sell porridge. These children already have their foot on the first rung of the commuter ladder.

St Leonards is also blessed with a minority brigade of pretentious yummy mummies with their spoilt, demanding offspring. They call hot milk a babyccino – it makes it sound more gourmet – I may allow myself an eye roll when my back is turned – depending on how the day is going and how yummily pretentious (foils!) we all are. However, business development analysis tells me that converts of the babyccino drinker are really future cappuccino drinkers in training – and therefore identifiable as my target market for the future. Perhaps I should reverse my thinking and put more energy into harnessing this market rather than performing a silent cross comparison between their childhood and mine. Flask.

Children that come in during the day should usually be hugged. Typically, they are on their way to London for a hospital appointment – some are routine – some far more serious – cancer, heart, rare conditions I am fortunate enough not to have to understand personally. Their parent's faces tell me all I need to know. What these little people have to endure is heart-breaking. The sicker the child the braver they seem to be. A stark reminder to us all that if we have health – then all other upgrades beginning with 'i' are really not important. I is for I forget to charge their parents for some of their items.

Surly Burly

'Large latte and can I charge my phone?'
'Sorry – no public socket at the Station.'
'But I'm out of charge.'

I must say he unnerved me a little the first time he came in, and the second, and the third. Built like the proverbial brick out-house with sleeves of tattoos on biceps that refused to be contained by his t-shirt. Bit scowly, bit unfriendly.

He was desperate for a phone charger socket. There is no public socket anywhere at the Station. That is not my responsibility and I have a strict policy that does not allow for the charging of anybody's phone within the unit. If you pick a lucky day and Tatz is working – and because she could not think of anything she would like less than to watch the battery power light on her phone fade to nothing – she will probably lend you her portable charger.

Surly Burly wanted a socket – I did not want a problem. It was a beautiful sunny day, I decided to bend my own rule. Phones need time to charge so I braved a conversation. I could see he spent hours in the gym and was a lover of all things protein, judging by the amount of money he spent in the gluten free, hug-a-tree, protein-loaded section of counter snacks. To my surprise, Surly Burly was in fact a British Weight Lifting junior coach. He told me about the programme that encourages youngsters to take up the sport. There is a certain amount of Lottery funding available. He was coaching a teenage girl who was showing considerable promise and phenomenal determination, sticking to a rigorous daily training schedule and diet. I have the utmost respect for determination and dedication – qualities I have successfully instilled in my own children. My respect for Surly Burly was lifted overhead.

The Olympics were still a very relevant topic – London euphoria hanging on. The popularity of a sport will fluctuate through the rankings according to the direction of the wind and the number of gold medals. Keeping the ribbons coming in means your sport will gain more funding as it rises to the top of the popularity stakes. Cycling had sped ahead to the top of the funding pyramid, whereas weight lifting had seen a demise, crushed by the weight of its own bar.

I handed him back his fully charged phone. Passionate about his sport, frustrated by money and fully supportive of all the bright young hopefuls – Surly Burly strode off towards the train with a sports massage book from the free shelf above the pew. I should add a sports related charity to the charity box section on the front counter.

Stone the Crows

CROWHURST – THE butt of an 'in' joke for people who commute back on the late London train. Does anyone actually live there? Philmore is in on the joke – assuring me it is a jaw dropping moment when somebody actually gets off the train at Crowhurst – worthy of carriage applause from anybody left awake – because the way back always seems so much further than the way there.

I escape up to London periodically – enjoying the change of scene for an evening. It surprises me how often I have spotted a regular on a very late train home – deprived of any kind of free time – Monday to Friday. Financially it must be worth it – or they would not do it – but from the perspective of balance – is it really? They remind me how lucky I am to be me – I love what I do – locally.

The train announcements of the stops en route to the birthplace of television bounce through the train tannoy – an upbeat recital of all the appealing stops along the line from Charing Cross to smug Wadhurst – after which the announcement gets slower and slower as it calls out all the villages, Stonegate, Etchingham, Robertsbridge, Battle …Crowhurst …West St Leonards … and then almost as an afterthought … St Leonards Warrior Square – not even trying to sell it to the crowd.

"The train now approaching Platform 1 is the 12.34 Southeastern service (blue train) to London Charing Cross calling at West St Leonards, Crowhurst …"

Crowhurst is an isolated village 5 miles north west of Hastings with a population of 891 – of which a tiny percentage take the train.

Please Use the Bin

THERE ARE SEVERAL provided on the Station platform, clearly visible, emptied regularly – all there for your convenience. What do you mean you're afraid of the giant killer seagulls that patrol the roof tops waiting for their chance to dive-bomb your pasty? Just use the bin. Please do not stuff yourselves full of food and drink on the bench outside, purchased from another outlet, and then lean your right arm in and attempt to shove your rubbish in my bin, partially all over the floor, and all over the bin lid. Do you really think I cannot see you? That arm has to be attached to someone. Please, please, no more nappies, or 'doggie' bags.

I suppose I would rather you put rubbish in my bin as oppose to no bin. Thoughtless individuals leave it blowing around outside making it the station staff's problem. If you are going to use my bin, please have the decency to get off your backside and use it properly.

For all those who cannot see the obvious – the great big white display container next to the grey rubbish bin under the shelf where the tea, coffee and stirrers live, clearly labelled on the front 'Hastings Independent', is not, whatever your view, a rubbish bin. It is for the free local newspaper – a favour I do for the local community. If the stand is empty – it means a new issue is imminent – so please – just use the bin.

"An ambulance has been called for an ill passenger on a train at Tunbridge Wells. Minor delays may occur to trains at the station as Platform 1 is currently blocked."

'Is there a toilet on the Platform?'

No point saying there will be one on the train as there is not only no toilet, but now there is also no train.

Ode to Harriet Harpie

I DON'T USUALLY work Saturdays. This particular one had been very busy – and mid-way through the day in walked Harriet Harpie.

"Get me an oat-milk latte – now."
I looked directly at her and said *"please."*

As I turned to make the drink she said *"Is there any chance you could be less sarky?"*
Today was the day. I put down the jug, turning to face her.

"That's it – I am not putting up with you any more – you are consistently rude to every single member of the staff – nothing is ever good enough for you – out you go – I don't want your money – we will no longer serve you."

"They are all liars! Are you fucking kidding me?"

"No."

"Because I wouldn't say please."

"Yes – good manners cost nothing – you have none – so good bye."

"But I need a coffee."

"Bye – Bye."

"Well done love" – said 'next in the queue'.

She stood outside the shop shouting to anyone who would listen – *"That bitch wouldn't serve me because I wouldn't say please."* Seb frequently and irritatingly reminds me, usually after I have tripped over his stuff that he left lying on the stairs, that the minute you start shouting, you have already lost the argument. I have to concede – he is absolutely right. Shout on then Harriet Harpie – I did it for me – I did it for the team. The coffee shop is a happier place.

Carpenter Diem

'Do you mind if I put some cards on the shelf?'

'Please do'

'Thanks. I'm on the tools – looking for work.'

Closing up on a dreary Monday afternoon, I was reflecting and considering everything and nothing while loading the dishwasher at the far end of the counter. I thought I was alone. I turned and jumped out of my skin. Magic Mike was leaning against the counter consuming all the space and the daylight. Skin head, thick head or bald head – I was not sure. Leather jacket, black eyes that I would not like to irritate – hands like shovels. Thug or prize fighter – too early to call it.

The metal grid outside the shop rattles as customers step on it when they enter the shop – it probably needs replacing. It is a relatively fool proof, incoming alert, unless someone strides over it. Like he had. Intentionally? Internal alarm bells were ringing. With only one way in or out, I had a potential stand-off situation.

He lifted his hands like a priest at a baptism, apologising profusely for making me jump. A Bermondsey boy, not a DFL. I asked him what he wanted. Silence followed silence. I am not afraid to front out an adverse situation – partly because my sprinting days are a dim and distant memory.

My silence had the edge and sheepishly he asked me if I could spare him a cup of tea. An unusual chancer – at St Leonards they tend to appear in pairs – one to distract while the other steals from the chiller. Magic Mike's jacket was expensive – an observation, not a judgement. Maybe his black eyes were troubled rather than angry. I gave him my Paddington stare – and to my own surprise – I handed him a tea on the understanding he paid it forward elsewhere.

Random acts of kindness happen both sides of the counter – usually from those you least expect it from. A young, motorbike happy chef from Lewes paid for a coffee for the man in front of him who was short of change. He paid for it with a wide smile and no agenda. Impressed by his integrity – I gave him an extra stamp on his loyalty card.

Magic Mike was a new arrival to St Leonards. A carpenter by trade – trawling the area for work. I hoped I was looking at a proud man down on his luck – but the jury was out. Proud men have been known to choke asking for a hand out – preferring to go without on their journey to breaking point. As the tea went in the pain came out – he sat on the pew and out came the confession.

He had come home early one day to find his girlfriend in bed with his neighbour. Resisting the temptation to paste him, he gathered up his little dog and tools and headed to the coast. Adultery can hit hard – I was pretty sure Magic Mike could hit harder and wondered how the neighbour really was. St Leonards is a good town to hide out in. He wanted to show me her photograph, but surprisingly his phone was out of charge. I plugged it in – the second time I have agreed to this – please do not assume it will open the floodgates for the entire travelling public to charge their phone at my expense.

I knew of a fit-out job coming up and checked out his working credentials. He was indeed a scenic carpenter, with a wealth of experience at Elstree Studios on huge film sets. Currently between films while waiting for the next one to start – just like an actor. He forgot to mention that the wealth of his experience comes predominantly from Westerns, which might explain why he is between films.

I made a phone call and a friend of mine reluctantly gave him a chance – while voicing a very clear suspicion to me that this would not end well for somebody. Sadly, he was right. Four days over budget, some dodgy receipts and a large bill for unauthorized supplies on account, together with an urgent requirement to get a plumber to repair the plumbing, Magic Mike turned out to be the most expensive cup of free tea I've ever given. What a shyster. If I ever see him again I'll probably launch a cup at him.

Catch me once – shame on me. Catch me twice it won't be nice. It won't be nice.

'Cup of tea?'
'Tea bag in or out?'
'In.'
'Catch.'

Donna

HER HAIR WAS bright blue, aviator glasses low down on her nose
and a huge smile. She called me darlin' in that over- familiar way.

Donna had her four children with her. They were on their way
to Butlins for a family holiday – an annual event – they had been
going there for years. I groaned to myself. Butlins would be my
idea of absolute hell. I would rather stay at home. I am sure there
are thousands and thousands of people who would shout me down
at the first opportunity and fair play to them. I hope they all enjoy
themselves.

I heard clonking and chinking in her bag as she knocked it against
the counter. The familiar sounds of passengers with booze for
consumption on and off the train. I laughed and made some flippant
remark about being set for a good time.

Donna was indeed set for a good time – this was to be their very
last family holiday together. Her cancer had started as breast cancer
– she fought, but five years later it had returned stronger and more
aggressive than ever. Now it was in her bones, her lungs and her
liver. I think it goes without saying that cancer impacts on all our
lives in some way. I lost a friend to breast cancer – I last saw her
sitting in the Lake District with a bandana on her bald head. She
didn't have the energy to walk but was determined to enjoy the

view. We think we have all the time in the world, but we just never know. Suddenly – we can be gone – so why do we take our days for granted? I did not know what to say – what is there to say? The harshest of blows. Smiling – she rummaged around in her bag and pulled out a couple of large bottles of Baileys – her favourite. Then I knew what was going in her black americano. Her blue hair the flag of brave spirit. I hope she had the time of her life.

Chapter 14

Satori to Nirvana

As LIFE CHANGES – so does my customer base. Relocation, children, working from home etc. Sometimes several months pass by and just when I think they have dropped off the radar permanently – they walk in unexpectedly. Sometimes regulars inform me that they won't be around for a while. I like the fact that they do – a bit like cancelling the papers and unplugging electrical equipment before going on holiday – a sign that I have become part of their every-day life.

In walked Large Marge. She looked amazing – hair done, make-up on – hefty, matching, pink leopard-print suitcases. *"Ello duck,"* she said, *"I'm off on my cruise ..."*

The train now arriving at Platform 1 is the 13.34 calling at St Leonards Warrior Square ... (blue train).

My satori moment rolled in with this train. I took a long, hard look at my reality – my own true nature. I have been running away my whole life – chasing rainbows, rebelling, fighting off entrapment, cutting off roots – shouting loudly about the negative constraints of limitation and restriction – moving from place to place – running for the hills at every opportunity. But I had not realised that I was running from myself. So, there could be no escape – because wherever I run – I take myself with me. You can only reinvent yourself on the surface. What lies beneath will haunt you – and if you don't like what you find there – you can either put a plaster on it – or you can get it by the throat and extinguish it.

Maybe it is time to stand still. I am happy here. Life is good – business is good – is there really any need to change it? The thought stopped me dead in my own tracks, rooting me to the coffee shop floor. I watched the passengers get on, the doors slide shut and the train head out through the next tunnel.

When I arrived on Platform 1 I had nothing. I was redundant, skint, worried, single and burdened by the heavy responsibilities on my shoulders. Without even knowing how, I suddenly had so much. By complete accident, I had arrived at a destination unknown. Connected to a community through coffee and a series of counter conversations with regulars and irregulars. Connected – accepting the unfamiliar sensation of belonging – while acknowledging there is a place for me in this community.

"Roberto!"
"I missed you – everything is alright sweetheart – I was a stubborn fool."
"I missed you too. Shall we pick up where we left off over a bottle of red?"
"Ab-so-lute-ly."

Rebellion Extinction

THE IRONY OF a sideways grin is that it tends to back fire. Rebellion is usually thought of as a liberating way of gaining independence. But in reality, the need itself to constantly rebel becomes an act of dependency. The dependency stems from a person having to do the opposite of what everyone else wants in order to define who they are. This is an incredibly frustrating discovery. 'I have met the enemy and it is me!' I have pushed enough boundaries and championed enough causes for the time being. I am paving the way for more moderate behaviour.

So, what am I really scared of?

Nirvana

My relationships have never gone well. Each one failed on its own particular merit because relationships are complex and their success or demise can never be attributed to one thing or one person. But what I have now established is a series of common denominators – and their presence is both undeniable and undesirable.

I am a perfectionist – as I have already explained – so it causes me considerable discomfort to admit that I am fundamentally flawed. With this admission comes complete acceptance that this does not make me a bad person. It may make me a complicated one – but that can be exciting if you are brave and like a challenge.

I realise that my adoption has wreaked havoc on my ability to form a stable relationship – I hate to admit that so publicly – because I pride myself on being strong and in control. The power of the subconscious and the supressed should not be underestimated. I can constantly object if I want to – but I am only damaging myself.

My birth mother disappeared off into the horizon – undoubtedly better for me on the one hand – but there is an argument to suggest that in doing so she inadvertently (fucked me over) abused me on an emotional level. I have all the symptoms of someone who suffers with a fear of commitment. Fear – the very thing I protest I do not suffer from – probably stemming from my early childhood needs being unmet – which in turn can cause attachment issues. My fear of relationships is really a fear of abandonment – a childhood trauma – which in turn could explain where my misophonia comes from.

Station Man Revisited.

HE WALKED INTO the coffee shop and I could see from his face that something was different. Time sweeps away some obstacles. Station Man had come back to St Leonards to find me. This time I was excited to see him – not fluttery – something new – something much deeper. I had missed him so much. We had tried to settle for friendship – but passions run high – so the friendship left with the lover.

Station Man was standing there – right in front of me in the coffee shop. Life had changed and he had come to tell me he was emotionally available and looking for commitment. But could I change?

My moment of truth. A man looking for serious commitment – for me the most terrifying kind. I have always been comfortable dodging emotional intimacy and deflecting attention from my own imperfections – usually while pointing out everybody else's – that's a Virgo trait – I can't blame my birth mother for everything! After all – there may be common denominators – but ultimately, we are all responsible for our own actions. I have chosen a lonely, hard road – and here I am at a T-junction. *"If things don't go right – go left."*

Station Man – he is so many things. His intuition startles me the most. His patience is endless – a lover not a fighter. He isn't looking for perfection – because to him I am perfect. I know I frustrate him – I frustrate myself. I make no apology – I am who I am – but I could try to be more accommodating – I find that easier to spell than 'open.' After all – is there another man on the planet who would bring me a coffee the second I open my eyes – and knowing he might gulp and aggravate my sensory perception – drink his outside? Or leave me a birthday surprise under my pillow – that I do not mention all day – and he doesn't mention because he knows that my birthday is a difficult day – when I just didn't discover it till bedtime. He is selfless –and whether I like it or not – he understands me and is not going anywhere. So, which one of us is really the catch?

Silently he held out his hand for me. I hesitated. Could I trust this? If I surrender then there are no battles to fight, nobody to fix and I will not know who I am. I choose to hang out with transgressors – they are safe to play with because we are two of a kind – guaranteed to let each other down as the cycle of abandonment repeats itself. Do I want to remain stagnant revisiting all the chapters of my life I keep promising myself never to return to? Or do I want to step on to a new platform with new destinations and ride a different train. My very own Hobson's choice – take it or miss it.

Unclaimed Baggage

MY COFFEE SHOP has an invisible sign that is staff-facing. 'Would you like counselling while you make my coffee?' After all, conversations are a two-way process. Through taking the time to listen to others – I have learnt so much more about myself.

We are all works in progress for different reasons – why should I be any different? I have let my subconscious fears rule my life – while all this time I believed it was me in control. I now understand why I am scared of commitment; am quick to move on; find emotional intimacy difficult; feel insecure and unworthy of love; find it hard to trust people; am hypersensitive to criticism; why I push people as far away from me as possible when they desperately want me to let them in. I didn't need a counsellor to figure all this out – I just needed a coffee shop and some counter conversations – saving myself a fortune in therapy fees! I feel a double espresso coming on.

This is all baggage that I do not want – so I am going to leave it behind – unclaimed lost property – as I walk away instead of running – setting myself free – because I am strong. I like a challenge.

The Alchemist

ROB MARSHALL IS a humanist and musical creative who helps out in the coffee shop when his guitar permits. A deep thinker who encourages me to think harder – he goes on his own journey of vision through sound. *"For me it is all about capturing energy as quickly as possible. When you feel that otherworldly something in the air – act with spontaneity."* Sound advice. An alchemist is a person who transforms or creates something through a seemingly magical process. Coffee is my elixir. Station Man is my alchemist.

Station Man was still standing there – hands out – accepting my strengths and my weaknesses. Understanding my fears well before I did – because he knows how to look deep. He always told me it would be alright in the end. Patience is his speciality – I know – I have tried his. He wants me to be able to feel vulnerable without needing to feel defensive. Station Man is in love with all of me. Slowly I will learn to trust love, as my life starts to settle and I accept that I have earned my own place in this society.

I walked quietly round to the less familiar side of the counter. There we stood – side by side – his hand in mine. He held it tight and together we crossed back over the line. I am at the break of my civil dawn.

Overlooking Life

THIS, THEN, IS life overlooked on Platform 1 – all the hidden stories, the loves, the losses, the comedy, the chancers, the strangers and the friends. This is the job I had never envisaged when I stepped on the first rung of my career ladder. Strangely, despite all my life experiences, this has become the job I value the most. I now realise that all the trepidation I felt when I arrived, determined and somewhat desperate, at St Leonards Warrior Square was a result of making a snap judgment about a place with my blinkers on. Today my blinkers are off and my eyes are wide open.

I had never given any thought to what life could be like off the rails somewhere between the counter and the next train. What started off as a few cups of commuter coffee has become so much more. The coffee shop on Platform 1 has given me the most fascinating, random, unexpected, predictable and invaluable insight into society. It continues to do this every single day. I am surrounded by ordinary people living extraordinary lives. Customers may be the same, orders may be the same, but no two days are ever really the same – for any of us.

St Leonards has given me an invaluable and multidimensional overview of life. These days I now respect the power of the underestimated, the understated, the unseen and the unspoken. I have repaid the loan but the wealth that I have accrued cannot be measured.

Every person is on their own unique journey and some journeys end sooner than others. We may sit in wary silence – believing we are anonymous strangers – shielding ourselves from interaction by hiding within our own private worlds. But whether we accept it or not – there will always be a connection – no matter how small.

What if ... we stopped for a moment to appreciate or contemplate the struggles surrounding the person next to us – or smiled, moved our bag, or just said a kind word? What if we didn't pass judgement based on what we think we see? Because we really have no idea and preconceptions are usually wrong. What if we took the risk and allowed ourselves to accept the rich gift of connection with strangers?

I have received these life changing lessons from the most unlikely of teachers in the most unusual classroom – the coffee shop on Platform 1.

"The train now approaching Platform 1 is ... My train."

CPSIA information can be obtained
at www.ICGtesting.com
Printed in the USA
BVHW040837040221
599297BV00019B/109